T.I.P.S. TO STUDY ABROAD
Simple Letters for Complex Engagement

The Letterwallahs, with Anu Taranath

ISBN-13: 978-0989626330 (Flying Chickadee)
ISBN-10: 0989626334

First printing, April 2014
Flying Chickadee
PO Box 30021, Seattle, WA 98113-0021
www.flyingchickadee.com
Write to author: tipstostudyabroad@gmail.com

Cover illustration and design © 2014 by Shahana Dattagupta, Flying Chickadee
Editing by Shirin Subhani and Shahana Dattagupta, Flying Chickadee
Interior photographs by Amy Hersh, Amy Hirayama, Annika Van Gilder, Brandon Maust, Fabiola Arroyo Lopez, Kelli Clark, Margaret Babayan, Nicole Okada, Olivia Lafond, Rukie Hartman

CONTENTS

Introduction 1

The Letters

    Thing 13

    Idea 43

    Person 75

    Self 99

Meet The Letterwallahs 115

Meet the Program Guides 121

Gratitude 122

Dear Reader Dear City of Bangalore, Capital of Karnataka State, South India Dear Study Abroad **Dear Kiddies** Dear Letters Dear Slow Dear Amy and Brandon Dear Go-Betweenness Dear Bangalore Friends and Colleagues Dear Reader **Dear City of Bangalore, Capital of Karnataka State, South India** Dear Study Abroad Dear Kiddies Dear Letters Dear Slow Dear Amy and Brandon Dear Go-Betweenness Dear Bangalore Friends and Colleagues **Dear Reader** Dear City of Bangalore, Capital of Karnataka State, South India **Dear Study Abroad** Dear Kiddies Dear Letters Dear Slow Dear Amy and Brandon Dear Go-Betweenness Dear Bangalore Friends and Colleagues Dear Reader Dear City of Bangalore, Capital of Karnataka State, South India Dear Study Abroad Dear Kiddies Dear Letters **Dear Amy and Brandon** Dear Go-Betweenness Dear Bangalore Friends and Colleagues Dear Reader Dear City of Bangalore, Capital of Karnataka State South India Dear Study Abroad Dear Kiddies Dear Letters **Dear Slow** Dear Amy and Brandon Dear Go-Betweenness Dear Bangalore Friends and Colleagues Dear Reader Dear City of Bangalore, Capital of Karnataka State, South India Dear Study Abroad Dear Kiddies Dear Letters Dear Slow Dear Amy and Brandon **Dear Go-Betweenness** Dear Bangalore Friends and Colleagues Dear Reader Dear City of Bangalore, Capital of Karnataka State, South India Dear Study Abroad Dear Kiddies **Dear Letters** Dear Slow Dear Amy and Brandon Dear Go-Betweenness **Dear Bangalore Friends and Colleagues** Dear Reader Dear City of Bangalore, Capital of Karnataka State, South India Dear Study Abroad Dear Kiddies Dear Letters Dear Slow Dear Amy and Brandon Dear Go-Betweenness Dear Bangalore Friends

INTRO

Dear Reader,

Hello and welcome! Have you ever found yourself traveling through faraway lands, wondering what makes us essentially the same or different from one another? When you meet new folks and visit new places, do you marvel at the variety of ways that people all around the world love, work, laugh, struggle and play? Even though travel can be exciting and eye-opening, spending time in a new cultural context can also make us yearn for ways to better understand our thoughts, feelings, and experiences.

This book addresses ideas that are at the heart of reflective global travel. *TIPS to Study Abroad: Simple Letters for Complex Engagement* offers a simple method to help travelers — students and tourists alike — reflect on how moving from one context to another invites questions about identity, society, and the meaning of travel itself. While leading University of Washington students on a study abroad program to India, I developed a letter-writing assignment. Each week I asked students to handwrite letters to a specific Thing, Idea, Person and Self (TIPS). Like many travelers abroad, my students experienced both unsettling and wonderful situations, and the handwritten weekly TIPS letters became a ritualized site in which they poured their curiosity, questions, frustrations, joys and insight. TIPS letters helped students productively process and make sense of their experiences. The practice of writing letters also helped my student travelers relate to the things, ideas and people of our host country in a more personal and intimate way.

Even though our letters are rooted in the context of my particular teaching, our program to India and the individual students (the *letterwallahs* or letter writers) whose voices you will soon read, we share *TIPS to Study Abroad* to inspire your own reflections about journeys and who we are through it all. What letters to Things, Ideas, People and Self might you too compose? Where might *TIPS to Study Abroad* take you?

Safe Travels,
Dr. Anu Taranath

* * * * *

Dear City of Bangalore, capital of Karnataka state, South India,

Thank you for holding my curiosity for so many decades. As a child I'd visit you and associate your winding streets and expansive trees with the voices of my relatives, or the special treats we'd eat together. My memories of you spoke to my heart. Later as I began to tiptoe outside of my own bubble, the questions flooded in. I still loved you, but now I also wondered: Who were you building yourself up for, and why? How did you negotiate your old and new and everything in between? How could you treasure your local beauty, rhythm or flavor while you also become global? And most importantly, could you offer a "good life" to your inhabitants? Could the people who call you home actually live well, and if not, why?

As a way to wrestle with these queries and understand better, I've brought my students to you for ten years so we can learn together. We crisscross your gullies and bear witness to your stories to begin to understand how the big words of development, activism, globalization, and social change affect small, ordinary lives.

Perhaps it's odd to be the subject of study, but dear Bangalore, your transition and growth from a relaxed gardened town to the current urban metropolis status you hold makes you especially vexing, especially interesting. Your information technology boom of the last 20-30 years itself warrants deep investigation, let alone your painful struggles with urbanization. My students and I try to see you as you are – competing heartbeats jostled up against one another. It appears to me that too many people want to own and rule you, and some just want you to be. My students and I focus on building relationships with local people who engage you intimately. Knowing that we are outsiders, we'd still like to connect our experiences of you to our lives in Seattle. Every so often, we do.

Thank you for hosting and teaching us,
a desi in the diaspora

* * * * *

Dear Study Abroad,

I like your premise very much. I too believe strongly in the merits of educational travel in order to learn about global similarities and differences. But I also think you've got some work to do. Please: Less congratulatory celebration for the numbers of students you transport around the globe. Please: More regard for *how* and *why* and *with what intellectual and emotional tools* these students move about in contexts dissimilar to their homes.

I hope that my continued engagement with you will shape you as much as it continuously shapes me and the students of our program. Cheers to this two-way relationship of transformation!

In solidarity,
AT

* * * * *

Dear Go-Betweenness,

I'm not sure if you are an actual word, but nevertheless, you are a star in my book. I try to practice you as I move between geographies, disciplines, cultures and generations. There's a nimble and kinesthetic feel to you as you take me from here to there, back and forth – not caught somewhere in the middle as we usually fear but reveling in that rich and indeterminate space. You help me loosen up to sliiiither and sliiiide. You serve as my guide. You are a pulse of sorts, a glimpse of truth beyond this or that, right or wrong. Thank you for showing me that even while holding passionate convictions, being aware of you is better than being stuck on one side or another.

Sincerely,
AT

* * * * *

Dear Letters,

It is funny to be writing a letter to a letter! You, my friend, are a thoroughly social genre. When we draw upon your long tradition and use your form to express ourselves with another, I see how connection is woven into your very form. Consider this: In what other literary category are both recipient and sender acknowledged, known, and held together between greeting and closing? You do not require one to be overly mushy (not even if you're a love letter!), but you also do not sport so-called academic objectivity. You ask us to frankly state ourselves, for another, and then proceed.

Did you know that for years I have used letter-writing in my classes as both an effective composition strategy and an alternative method of study and analysis? I've found that students love using you to express ideas that sadly otherwise seem outside the academic realm. Perhaps students are able to experience you as more personal and intimate, as better able to hold emotions and vulnerability better than more traditional forms of academic writing, wouldn't you say?

I'd like to think that each time we pen our names as a signatory, we scoot a little closer toward our recipient. You are so juicy and versatile!

Thanks for all your hard work,
AT

* * * * *

.

Dear Slow,

In a fast-paced world buzzing along capriciously, you are clearly a less glamorous second. Many think of you as an impediment to progress or inherently lazy. I wonder: Does that make you feel bad? You are, after all, what helped that underdog tortoise unexpectedly make it to the finish line before the speedy, puffed-up hare, right? You must find great pride that lately, a grassroots movement has grown around you. The "slow movement" is now an actual force, with supporters promoting slow food, slow parenting, slow cinema, slow gardening, slow architecture, slow everything. Slowies simultaneously advocate for less and more: less hustle and bustle, more flavor and savor.

I think you're a great idea for education, too. Can we please slow things down in the classroom? Start an educational movement that prioritizes meaningful relationships between people as they learn and teach? Let's call it slow pedagogy. Slow pedagogy turns away from corporate modes of education—including teaching to the test, banking methods of instruction, and a model that makes consumers out of learners. Instead, slow pedagogy makes time to get to know students, and crafts learning that matters. It builds on the work of many educational progressives, and who knows, could very well enact a cultural shift to make us better collaborators and community members.

I know that what I am suggesting is an ideal. But if the slow foodies have been able to transform the dreaded "What can I throw together for dinner?" panic into an experience to treasure, surely we can do something similarly meaningful in the classroom?

Unhurriedly,
AT

* * * * *

Dear Kiddies,

Can you believe that the idea for what's in this book came from us, two Kiddies and an Ammi? Thank you for giving me great ideas that I can use with my students! Every night before I put you both to bed, we talk about three specific things: which wonderful *jenna* we interacted with today (*jenna* is "people" in our home language Kannada), which wonderful feeling we were happy to feel, and which wonderful thing we were glad to have experienced. Every single night each of us gets a chance to share our "*Jenna*, Feeling, Thing," and we've done this for so long that people close to us know about it too. This is how my colleagues and co-conspirators Amy and Brandon helped me come up with the idea for TIPS! I love "*Jenna*, Feeling, Thing" for warming us with gratitude in a personalized way, and hugging us close together in a sweet squeeze.

If it were night now and you both asked me to share my "*Jenna*, Feeling, Thing" for the day, I'd say my Jenna are the wonderful people in my life, Feeling is I am lucky to have a job I love, and one specific Thing I appreciated today was my steaming cup of *chai*!

Love and smoochies,
Ammi

* * * * *

Dear Amy and Brandon,

Thank you both for all the fabulous discussions and great ideas we've shared over the years. Your deep commitment to radical and transformative pedagogy has been incredibly encouraging to me as I have experimented, retooled and stretched myself both in and out of the classroom. Both of you are now part of our family, well-loved by me for your friendship and collegiality, well-loved by my kids for your playfulness and affections.

This round kitchen table here at my home, at which I sit to write to you now, has featured significantly in much of our work, no? We have drunk a lot of *chai* and eaten a lot of *chapatis* sitting together, laptops and coloring books and Lego bricks comfortably cluttering our space. Our kitchen table conversations have seeded some wonderful ideas like developing *"Jenna, Feeling, Thing"* into the teaching tool of TIPS. I am so glad to dream and plan and work with you both. Can't wait to see what we come up with next!

with love,
anu

* * * * *

Dear Bangalore Friends and Colleagues,

How to convey our appreciation and affections to you all? A "thank you for all you have done for us" message might be heartfelt, but the words themselves are too generic to seem all that significant.

Let us then make some small statements that in their truthfulness, make big meaning:

We didn't change the world,
but
You taught us well.
We made you laugh.
We hope the space we created together felt rich with possibility and curiosity.
We think of you often.
and
We join you in doing good work here in our own communities.

And yes, thank you for all you have done for us.

Gratefully and respectfully,
The Letterwallahs and AT

* * * * *

Markets **Journal** Dogs Wang's Kitchen restaurant UTC noises outside my window Details **Dhoti** Intestines **Garment industry** House cut in half SIM card Water Cold sore Temple **Chai breaks** Journal that I got from Amy, Brandon, and Anu **Curd rice** Coffee beans Landfill Injuries Time of the month Umbrella in Shivajinagar **Short hair** Business card **This ole pair of Nikes** Soap operas Sickness Tropicana guava juice box Acne Biscuit wrapper Details **Terrace** Malls Stolen cell phone **Fingernails** NGOs Lalbagh on Independence Day Water Chai breaks **Middle ground** Plastic Mosquito bite scars Sidewalk Skeleton in the wall Props **Bag made to commemorate our time here** Dancing on the bus Moist sheets Burning feet Birthday Pooping Fatphobia **Auto rickshaws** Scholarship Details Pen and paper Responses to letters Gobi Manchurian Things that I miss **Amar Chitra Kathas** Homestay home Mall Migraines Things that I have bought to take back home with me to people I care about **Paneer curry** Bangalore Potty spray device Washing machine Blue sky **World/planet/earth** Western pop music in Bangalore Central Headphones Star in the sky that shelters the bed in which I sleep Drinking water Queerness Rickshaws **Plastic water bottle** Central Mall Mall ISD telephone in the Mobility **Trees of Bangalore** India Giving back Cafeteria Hospitality Royal Meenakshi Mall Walls Fan Rickshaw in the rain **Trees above us** Journal Markets **Fat Monkey** Period, PMS, and sore breasts Sidewalk Markets Dancing on the bus **Pooping** Tropicana guava juice box Things that I miss Pen and paper Western pop music in Bangalore Lalbagh on Independence Day Migraines Washing machine Business card Mosquito bite scars Headphones Star in the sky that

THING

Dear World/Planet/Earth,

There is a sad, romantic idea I get when I think of you, Planet Earth. The image of you from space is so shudderingly still – unreal, even, and your grooves and seas appear so comfortingly familiar. I always thought I would know you up close, as well, just as when I zone in on well-worn specks of cities, I can recollect tangible memories to create meaning. Yet, you're different in the pictures, because no speck is alike, and all too similar at the same time.

There is no broadened context here, at this speck called Bangalore, on this blot called India. I can no longer trace lines of imagination that lead me to reels of green jungles and spice markets at dawn, for I am standing on a sidewalk which drops off suddenly into a rushing flow of grey liquid swimming with garbage, and the smell of urine is giving me a headache. This is new in the wrong way, and even the familiar unsettles me as well. The empty political speeches, the feeling of rain falling on my neck, the dry sensation of dust on my feet. Things feel the same, even when they shouldn't. So I try to draw a line back to home. But it's night there, and I cannot explain that I have seen a woman holding a crying child and a pan for coins, because even if I had been able to tell what I had seen, it would have been a strange dream upon waking. I cannot hold both dawn and dusk in my heart at the same time – I cannot draw lines from one speck to another without seeing and feeling images from both, and knowing that while one is in shadow, the other is in sunlight.

For being round, earth, you are painfully unequal. You separate the familiar and the beloved with lashes of time, and hide away so much in the sleeping realm of the unknowable. What can be known is layered, and always staggered by the rotation of your unfathomable shape. I cannot hold both halves, I cannot even see them simultaneously. Your only sense of justice is to keep on spinning.

Rebekah

* * * * *

Dear Journal,

We used to be close; you knew all of my secrets. You kept all of my ideas bound to existence but I seem to have lost your pages scribbled with ink, just as I have lost my desire to mark you with meaning. I feel like if I were to write in you every day, you would find my expressions useless and mundane. What is the point of being able to recall anything, if you don't know what's worth remembering?... I think I feel ambivalent towards you because I have spent so much time trying to forget things instead of remember them.

I feel like you would be depressing if I wrote about my thoughts in you. Everybody writes in you but somehow you are such a special and different creation from each of us. You frustrate me because you are a reminder that I don't even make sense to myself. You can make me feel awkward. You make me wonder if my thoughts or expressions are worth remembering. I don't want to give you a simple commentary of my day because you deserve so much more than that.

You scare me a little bit. I don't want to look back someday at today and recall my dreams and ambitions as some crazy idea that only seemed to reach reality through the tip of my pen. Or maybe you scare me because you are more reflective than a mirror and you show me a part of myself I don't like to look at.

Bianca

* * * * *

Dear Poop,

I love pooping. Yes, this letter will be about pooping. Interestingly, I find that I like talking about pooping just as much, if not more, than the action itself. Maybe I enjoy the process more than most, or maybe I was raised in an environment that encouraged discussing it (Thanks mom). Either way, I think there is something truly valuable in talking about poop. Everybody poops, but not everyone talks about it. I have found that whether or not people like to admit it, write about it, or even think about it, poop is something that unites everyone. Your race and gender don't matter. Everyone is equal under the ceramic rule. Everyone poops. Your class does not matter, your caste does not matter, and your socio-economic status does not matter.

Or does it?

I am noticing that something is different here, both in practice and equality. First off, at home after I go through the often rigorous process of, you know, I generally feel relieved, relaxed, and happy. But here, that quickly fades as I remember I still need to do the whole water-hand-bum-wash thing. In addition though, I have noticed the different types of toilets or lack thereof. Women have infinitely fewer, if any, public toilets. The toilets in the institute are much simpler than those in our houses, which are simpler than mall toilets with toilet paper. Though no toilet compares to the hole in the ground at Mr. Mallesh's home. That is simplicity and practicality.

This is all to say that my preconceptions do not stand up to the truth. While all poop is the same, not all facilities are equal, and that says a lot about a society's hierarchies.

Marcello

* * * * *

Dear Fingernails,

I am unused to your length and texture. On an average day during the school year, I spend about 67% of my waking hours gnawing on you nervously, scraping to the cuticle, driven by the mindless habit of anxiety. For the past week, I have been catching myself before biting. I remind myself of the new germs I will be putting in my body, and the recent bathrooming technique which puts my hand in places it doesn't usually go. It's a strange feeling, halting my nail biting. What is different about Bangalore in comparison to Seattle that inhibits me from biting my nails?

My brain is pumped full of warnings against infectious diseases, malaria, encephalitis, dengue, sunstroke, dehydration, and, of course, sexual assault. Things don't seem to be exactly as how I was told they would be. The microbes my fingernails seem to be nesting have been giving me unpleasant flutters in my stomach, and the dirt gathers with a fantastic intensity. Still, I feel no different on a fundamental level.

People are people, despite our different customs and lifestyles. Germs are germs, dust is dust, and one community struggling for existence is essentially the same as another. So I am picking at my nails. I am trying to navigate what constitutes dangerous dirt, and what makes scum under my nails on one half of the world so much more threatening than the other half. The germs are real, my sickness is real, and there are things that could end up under my nails which I am not used to seeing, let alone accidentally chewing on. But still, dirt is dirt, and what it contains can be changed and contextualized. So I will keep picking, and not biting, and try to understand what is suddenly so strangely at my fingertips, and how it will affect and react in my own system.

Rebekah

* * * * *

18

Dear Trees of Bangalore,

I understand why Bangalore is known as the garden city of India. You are beautiful. Everywhere I look is a different type of tree, a new trunk or leaf design, growing up and out in ways I've never seen before. Your bark is smooth and rough, your trunks are long and skinny and short and fat and short and skinny and long and fat. You line streets, grow between stairways, influence building shapes, and fill up parks. From the polluted streets you offer refuge, creating oases of oxygen within the Bull Temple's garden or Cubbon Park. You give us shade to rest under, fruit to eat, and the breath that keeps us alive; what more could we ask for? Today when my stomach ached, your coconut's water soothed me. Last night when I missed home, your pomegranate seeds reminded me. When my thoughts seemed to overwhelm me, you gave me shade and birds' songs to soothe me. I feel blessed to share the earth with you. I'll leave you with a poem I read a few nights before leaving on this trip, and hope these few words will suffice:

Trees – Joyce Kilmer

I think that I shall never see
A poem lovely as a tree.
A tree whose hungry mouth is prest
Against the earth's sweet flowing breast;
A tree that looks at God all day,
And lifts her lovely arms to pray;
A tree that may in summer wear
A nest of robins in her hair;
Upon whose bosom snow has lain;
Who intimately lives with rain.
Poems are made by fools like me,
But only God can make a tree.

Sincerely,
Simon

* * * * *

Dear Curd Rice,

    We have come so far in these last 2 weeks! Do you remember the first time we met? Do you remember the strange awkwardness I felt at your sight, your smell, your sour taste, your touch? I recoiled as I felt that uncomfortable coolness transfer through my fingers. I felt I would never grow accustomed to your foreignness, just like so many other faces of the Bangalore I have come to see and know. Yet there I sat, last night, LOVING you. I have become quite fond of everything about you. Yes, you are "good for digestion". And yes, I have grown to enjoy your cooling touch on my lips, tongue, and throat. But there's something more, something that truly contradicts that initial reaction. Last night I realized it was all different.

    After scooping steaming rice onto my plate, I spooned you 3 times onto that pile. Then, after a moment's preparation, I shoved my right hand into your contradicting nature. Suddenly, I felt the hot steam of the rice clash with the soothing chill of the curd and meet in the battleground of my fist. I knew I shouldn't but I squeezed the fist of rice anyways, letting the temperature equilibrate between my fingers as the sloppy mix oozed over my knuckles. Then, after enjoying the beautiful texture of the course, I began to eat.

Your story, our story really, is just one example exemplifying the way I have become accustomed to many 'different' things in India. Some have surprised, some appalled, but the majority of the things to which I have become accustomed have simply numbed me. The trash in the street is no longer appalling, it just is. The smell of raw sewage is no longer shocking, but rather it's disgustingly normal. The child tugging at my sleeve still pulls on my heart, but it is more gentle than ferociously heart-wrenching as it once was. What does it say about me that I have gotten used to so much of the newness that I experienced here? I would like to think that I have not stopped questioning the contradictions I see. But, it is also quite reasonable to think that I have internalized many things to be 'the way it is here.'

Is that what it looks and feels like to see through another lens? Is it as simple as getting used to different things, seeing different things as normal? And if so, then if you allow atrocities to become 'normal', does that mean they are no longer atrocious? The question I guess I am asking myself is "How can I tell the difference between accepting the differences of another culture, and adopting the failures, blindness or inability to address problems of a culture?"

Can a foreigner ever accurately analyze the shortcomings of another culture? What does it mean that much of what shocked me 2 weeks ago now crashes weakly against my emotional armor? Am I adapting healthily to a new environment, or ignoring what might/does upset me? Honestly, I don't want to live a life where I am constantly accosted by my surroundings, because I can't. The way I can deal with this is to compromise: I will pledge to never stop questioning why the customs surrounding me exist, why things are the way they are. Perhaps I could take the latter promise with me when I return to America, home.

Marcello

* * * * *

Dear Middle Ground,

If I had ten rupees for every time someone has mentioned you (or "balance" or "compromise") over the course of this program, I would be rich.

I've heard you described as a safe place, a hard place, an uneasy place, a "wishy-washy" place, a political place, a desirable place, and a useless place. You are often used as a conclusion when discussing difficult/complicated issues: "There's no right answer, you just have to find a balance and live with the contradiction". You are also presented as a question: "We have these models/modes of thinking. What would the 'middle ground' look like?" I love your versatility.

In my experience, you have often been a source of comfort, but I am beginning to realize that this is only because I have been mistaking you for a kind of "neutral zone". I am the kind of person who can often understand and empathize with both sides of an issue, so I tend to treat you like a neutral space where the two sides do not come into conflict. I see now that you are actually full of tension and inherently political, and that any agreement developed in your space will be a hard-earned compromise.

With this in mind, I will be making some changes in the way I relate to you. You will no longer be an escape or an easy solution to a complicated problem. I will learn to embrace the conflict and hold the tension in my mind. Huge steps.

Let's see where they take us.

Nicole

* * * * *

Dear Plastic Water Bottles,

I don't know which one of you to address, as there are too many of you at this point. At first, I really made an effort not to abuse you. I reused my first water bottle the whole first week, but I kept dropping it in the street, along with the bottle cap, and I don't know what kinds of things it was really falling into. Also, it started to smell funny. So I took a bottle from a dinner at a restaurant. I figured I could probably go through one per week. But then there was the problem of where to refill it, so the bottles began to accumulate.

Every restaurant we go to, there are piles of empty and half-empty bottles that fill up the tables. We can talk and talk about the destruction and pollution of our environment, and how water bottles play such a powerful role; corporations who force communities into buying bottled water while tap water is unusable, all the things we can talk and fret and make ourselves feel so righteous over, while at the same time we have no choice but to play along with it.

It is so easy for us to proudly and loudly "live sustainably" in Seattle, where the highest quality water to be found is flushing our toilets and cleaning our gutters. But here, it is not so simple. Basic needs become something one must be aware of and even have to purchase at a damaging cost. All these things we know already, we talk about them at home and see them here. But now, it is settling in the pit of my stomach. I watch my own cost of existence grow in piles at restaurants and fill bin after bin of garbage. Talking does nothing when reality can't match it. Plastic is excessive, unnecessary, and convenient. It eats away in such small increments that the results of consumption are incalculable and massive. So it is with all things, luxury is careless and necessity is expensive. How could we ever return to a world without plastic bottles?

Rebekah

* * * * *

Dear Garment Industry,

This letter is dedicated not only to the garment industry as a general entity, but to the individual clothing companies that comprise to make what the garment industry is today.

I am writing to inform corporations like Nike, Adidas, H&M, GAP, Walmart, American Eagle, Old Navy, etc. that their yearly visits to factories in India/around the world are fake and staged. I know that may be a pretty strong statement, but it is necessary for you to TRULY know what is happening. When you visit the factory, you may notice that proper safety procedures are in place, like masks and safety glasses worn, and all facilities (including the bathrooms) may look clean and spotless. This is just a show and is not a true reflection of the conditions that the workers are working in. In reality, the factory bathrooms are hardly usable during the normal workweek and safety materials are never distributed. The factory puts on a show and you, for the most part, take it all in as the truth. The leaders of your companies that visit the factories do not know what it is like to live on less than minimal wage, much less working in hazardous working conditions.

We got the opportunity to speak with 3 very humble and hardworking garment workers and the 3 messages they wanted you to hear and consider are:

1. To increase their salaries (the average garment worker earns ~193 rupees/day... equivalent to $3/day)

2. To provide safer facilities (a basic human right), and

3. For production targets to be more manageable (it's so crazy how work can range from having no work and being sent home to having a lot of work and working tireless hours and sleepless nights).

On that note, it's hard to take a stand and boycott your products, because I know I will only be destroying jobs abroad, but at the same time how do we stop these evil things (salary and facility inequalities/abuses) from happening without boycotting and/or just being a conscious 'citizen' of society?

It's hard to say and I'm not sure if we have an answer yet. The garment workers have planted a seed and created change by sharing their stories. I am writing to share their story, and hopefully you will listen and consider making changes for the livelihoods of millions of men and women abroad.

Sincerely,
Fabiola

* * * * *

Dear this ole' pair of Nikes,

If it hadn't rained this morning I would never have worn you. If I couldn't find my socks I would never have worn you. But I did find my socks and it did rain this morning and so I did walk with you to class in front of a panel of women who may have been the ones who stitched that Nike swoosh onto your face. While the panel of garment workers shared their experiences, I worked my shoes as far back beneath my chair as possible, shamed and embarrassed of being named.

I know we all participate in the consumer/producer/worker relationship, but your swoosh separated me from the group more than my H&M shirt or Puma socks. You were the last Nike product I ever purchased and I should thank the women on the panel because their colleagues did an undeniably fantastic job. I just checked where you were made... turns out you were made in Vietnam. For the moment I am relieved. Thank God these women didn't make my shoes. Then again these women don't want shipment orders to stop completely, they just want fair and equitable working conditions: reasonable demands, increase in salary, and better working conditions. Their wants are no different than those required in the US. I wanted to ask if they felt any connection with the consumer or the shopping mall where their clothes were being sold a million miles away.

When I see that a shirt is made in India I imagine a stereotypical image of a mother of five sewing my shirt in a dimly lit room. Does she imagine me? So how do I manage to be an ethical shopper? I can't just choose with my dollar. No, as a consumer I need to change, along with the buyers, producers, and garment workers. I love you Nike but I don't think you will change.

Chris

* * * * *

Dear Fat Monkey,

Fat monkey I saw
Who captured all of my heart
I think I love you

Now, you may think it strange that a foreign passerby like me is so fond of a monkey like you. But I can explain.

Monkeys are rare in Seattle. You were the first monkey I encountered here. You fulfilled my orientalist hopes of finding exotic animals in India.

You are a chubby monkey. As a kid, I myself was chubby and I felt quite awkward about the whole ordeal. Even now, especially when I'm in new situations, I feel uncomfortable about my body and its size. Maybe you are just really cute, but maybe your size makes me feel better about mine.

And then there is your "adventure factor." Your kind has a reputation for being dangerous, and your friend had just stolen a mango from the man next to me. So I think I enjoy the rebellion and sense of risk.

Why a photo? With a photo, I can remember our encounter forever. I can show everyone how exciting my trip to India was. I can upload it to Facebook and be superficially validated by the number of "likes" you glean.

Monkey, the truth is, I think you're just what I need. You are one part expectation, one part adventure, one part memory, one part cool. Lately I've been taking things very seriously, and I need to laugh more. I need to enjoy little things like this picture of you.

So, thank you fat monkey. I love you.

Kelli

* * * * *

Dear Amar Chitra Kathas,

You are the only comic books I read as a child, and one of the only Indian/Hindu things I enjoyed before college.

Little did I know that you contain some very controversial material. Laxmi Ma'am blew you into pieces in just ONE morning. And with you, my childhood turned black. Just kidding, that's overdramatic. But I did feel betrayed by you. Your pretty drawings made Sita's exile to the woods seem normal. How weird is it that I bought you (Two Sons of Rama) just days before Laxmi Ma'am's lecture. I used to think all women were respected in Hinduism. But that turned out to be SO-NOT-TRUE. The stories of Sita and Draupadi are ones I've heard numerous times before, read in books, and watched in movies. The old fashioned movie about the Pandava brothers played often in our house. The treatment of women and sequence of events seemed totally normal to me. But the way Laxmi Ma'am told it, it blew my mind. My mind has never busted like that. A part of me wanted to quickly run up there and cover her mouth. That's how RADICAL and MIND BLOWING and DANGEROUS her ideas are. She was challenging some very core stories in Hinduism.

It made me really ashamed to have played into that culture/ way of thinking. There isn't anything acceptable about a woman having to walk into fire to prove her chastity or anything else. How did I not see that before?

But Laxmi Ma'am didn't leave me completely shattered and without answers. She said that these are INTERPRETATIONS that can be changed and re-examined. She offered alternative explanations. I look forward to exploring some of these texts. While I'm not extremely religious, my family has strong ties to Hinduism. I'd like to create a healthy relationship with it. The beauty of Hinduism is the amount of freedom it gives to practice and interpret it. I'll take full advantage of this. That way, when I pass you down to my children or godchildren, I can offer different explanations or give other views on the stories.

<3 Divya

* * * * *

Dear Chai Breaks,

Where have you been all my life? I have only been here for one week, and I am already growing to love you! You occur at all the right times, when I need some time to catch up with my classmates or when I need some time to let our discussions from class sink in. These kinds of coffee breaks are not common in the U.S. – getting coffee is either a scheduled date or it is a fast-paced stop on the way to school or work. I really have been appreciating the space you give me every day to relax and process.

We need more of you in this society that is speeding up every day. I don't give myself enough of these thoughtful breaks in Seattle. I am always moving quickly from class to work to a club meeting to another event. There isn't anything like you built Into our daily schedules, so I guess I will just have to start making time for you! I will treasure the relaxation you bring us during these next few weeks in Bangalore, and keep it in mind when I return to my much faster paced lifestyle. Thank you for reminding me to slow down.

Love,
Olivia

* * * * *

Dear Dhoti,

You are the coolest, queerest, bravest, and sexiest article of clothing I have ever worn. I love the idea of a single cloth being so dynamic – you could be like a skirt or shorts or pants or something else altogether. You are so radical. You make me radical.

You are the first article of *desi* clothing I bought here and on the second to last day. I was so worried and felt so much shame about gender, size, *desiness*, but when I saw you there on a mannequin waiting for me, you seemed like the ideal solution to my anxiety.

I had to overcome this sense that *desi* clothes were meant for *desis* and not me. There was such a gaping disconnect for me in terms of gender and diaspora, and you bridged it. Your intricacies were awe-inspiring to others and a source of pride for me at the end-of-the-program party. You are such a beautiful reflection of something I love about India – creative survival. In a place of extreme disparities, those in the camp of "have-nots" have survived when they weren't meant to in really amazing ways. You are something versatile and complex, derived from scarcity or simplicity – a single cloth. Here this might also look like a family of five on a two-wheeler or a wall being used as a urinal (just kidding!). There are so many ways folks here have used the simple/limited to make or do something intricate.

You are fabulous and you make me feel so whole. I love you! My mom thinks you are "low-class" but I think you are so hi-fi! I want to wear you all the time!

Love,
Sasha

P.S. How do I go to the bathroom when I am wearing you? Without getting you all nasty?

* * * * *

Dear Short Hair,

I love you. Not only are you practical and easy to wash, but in surprising ways, you are doing me political favors.

Last night on the way back, the rickshaw driver thought that I was a boy—not only a boy but my roommate's son. Would that moment of hilarity have been possible without you?

I spent a while thinking about why this was so funny to me. It's not that I want to shame the driver, who took a two-second look at someone who was sitting directly behind his head in a dark rickshaw and happened to jump to the wrong conclusion. I'm also not offended that someone would mistake my gender—I don't think how I look is shameful or that there is shame in being another gender. What's funny to me is having something I consider fundamental to my identity interpreted in a way different than how I see myself. And it comes from realizing that how I am perceived changes how I feel in a situation.

When I thought that he might think I was a boy, I felt immediately more empowered in the situation. I suddenly felt like this was *great*, that I could go more places, be more respected, bargain more ruthlessly, and feel safer. I realized that even though I didn't consciously think about it, I perceived myself as helpless when I knew that everyone saw me as a girl. This also seemed absurd to me. Why should short hair, some baggy clothes and poor lighting grant me more or less power? It seems wrong that my same physical features can put me arbitrarily in one category or another depending on who is looking, and where they think I belong.

This illusion will probably never happen again, and so, short hair, you aren't going to be my meal ticket. After all, I have to speak eventually, and I have a feminine voice. Nevertheless, thank you for opening up this experience for me. Thanks for letting me express who I am, and for occasionally letting me switch categories.

I love spending time with you.

Marie

* * * * *

Dear Tree above us,

Sitting underneath you, I am warmly welcomed by the women in the federation, a group of women that fights for women rights in their own local rural community. You are so lucky to be the Tree that provides shelter and a place of meeting for these women.

I think these women have given me a new insight into what activism means. Usually when I think of activism, I picture a big movement that mobilizes hundreds of people. In reality, activism can be small things that we do every day that impact our community. These women are doing an amazing job juggling two seemingly contradicting roles in their society, from housewife to activist.

They stand up and speak out for women's rights in issues such as child marriage. They are very courageous and outspoken when facing families and men in their community. Although they live in a small town in India, I find them to be radical people doing amazing work. They show that people living in rural areas are not backward. They are thinking about the same issues as people in urban areas. Instead of studying these issues, they are actually acting on them, which is even better. I hope you continue to thrive and grow as you symbolize the foundation and strength of the federation for me.

Love,
Vinnic

* * * * *

Bangalore 2013

Dear Bag made to commemorate our time here,

A feeling of such immense warmth filled my soul when Brandon and Amy revealed they were not in class this morning because they were picking you up. I held you with joy as Brandon described finding the organization which ethically produced you and Amy described her design process. Would I appreciate you if you were not, as Brandon said, "the definition of 'fair trade,'" or if Amy had not so artfully drawn the thali you wear on your face? Regardless, it is so silly that you may mean so much to me for years to come. You are, after all, just a couple of pieces of fabric stitched together. Indeed, it is silly that a material object like you can mean so much to anyone, but I guess humans can love even inanimate items for their sentiment.

I like you for your symbolism and appreciate the thoughtfulness behind your genesis. The image on your face—the cartoon thali

Amy drew— conveys the "diversity" of this group. Everyone here brought such vibrancy to our collective experience. I could not have imagined a better way to sum up this program other than with that thali which you display on your tan, woven fabric. This group was indeed like a meal: flavors and spices sprinkled throughout, distributed in different ways and taken in different combinations. The discussions which we synthesized and built our foundational frameworks upon moved us all toward understanding, but they would not have been so wonderful had not such radically different perspectives been present throughout the program. This program was not an excuse to hang out in Bangalore as the "Bangalore 2013" cohort. No, it was an opportunity to cultivate my understanding of justice, humanity, and myself.

Bag, I will cherish you, I will! But your presence will remind me that time is fleeting and that memories seem to matter only when they can materialize into trinkets or souvenirs. As much as I will love you, I will value my memory more. Thank you for existing, but I will not need you to reflect upon this moment in time.

Love,
Margaret

＊ ＊ ＊ ＊ ＊

Dear Auto Rickshaws,

You are awesome, seriously. Though your drivers overcharge me, leave me out in the rain, get lost, and take back-roads at night that scare me, you remain awesome. Why? Because the mobility and independence you provide are amazing.

I can hail you from pretty much anywhere in the city and, with enough patience/money/coaxing, go anywhere else in the city. You are way way cheaper than a car. You can fit up to like six people. And I don't have to worry about parking. There is really no adventure like you. You give mobility to women, the young, some of the poor, and the elderly. I feel like a super-woman when I hail you on my own, negotiate your fare (*meter hakki!*), and then let you take me wherever I want. Though your open sides expose me to dust, wind and pollution, I get to see the city in a way one can't in a bus, plane, shoes, car, etc. You don't hog space.

It would be cool, though impractical, if you existed in the US. How many more people would become at least partially mobile? How much time and money would we save? How would this affect our economy and environment?

I'll miss your rumbles when I go back.

<3 Divya

* * * * *

Dear Paneer Curry,

You were the last meal that I had in Bangalore. You were also the best meal. Asima auntie cooked it just for us because she wanted our last meal to be a home-cooked meal. A couple of weeks ago, I casually mentioned that you were my favorite Indian dish. So I was really touched to see that she remembered.

With you in my stomach, I had the most emotional car ride of my life as she drove us to the metro stop. Auntie sang us a song with sentimental lyrics. We talked about saying goodbye to people we love. When she dropped us off, she got out of the car and hugged each one of us tightly. We looked at each other, avoided glances and looked sideways as our tears stood behind our eyes. When we finally parted, I lost all control and cried in the middle of the road.

It's been eight hours since I ate you, and I haven't eaten anything since. But I'm still feeling full. That's how I feel about this whole trip. I feel full. My brain is full, and my heart is full. You are just one of many examples of the incredible warmth, care, and love that I've been showered with in Bangalore from street vendors, rickshaw drivers, activists, servers, random pedestrians, host family , and speakers. I'm going to be hungry in a couple of hours, but I know that you'll keep my heart full and warm for a long time to come.

Sincerely,
Minjung

* * * * *

Dear terrace,
Dear rain,
Dear padlocks and bolts,
Dear scarcity and surplus,
Dear homesickness,
Dear loneliness,
Dear laughter,
Dear red, cloudy, fading sky,

When rain falls, the power fails.
My host mother sits with a single light for her reading
lest the light for the evening run dry. I'd thought
electricity was endless. A faulty knob in the
upstairs bathroom drains 750 liters of precious water
from the tank and this put-upon woman gazes up and
says "It's so sad."

Of all things, a cold puts me away
for days. I shiver under the awning and
think of the ironic parting gift of wool
socks tucked away in a drawer at home.

Gazing off the terrace to the other
endless houses at dusk is beautiful.
Monsoon season.
The sky falls around me.

Home. Things I miss. Things. The red broom,
the disinfectant spray, the keys in my right hand. The road
bike saddle under my ass. The silent freeway. The place I own.
The place I belong to. The manners that mean something.
Chris cries, "Nothing is the same here!"
Even the fruit flies are different.

The city is a spatial and sensory
manifestation of a panic attack. The
screaming horns, locals staring,
sewage, exhaust, treacherous sidewalks,
the thick, sour smell of trash burning.
Cortisol surges. I don't sleep.

At the same time it doesn't feel so strange,
sitting in this blue plastic chair rather than my brown
sofa. Am I more out in the world now than there,
at home when I am pinned under my own darkness,
on the days I stay in as if locked in?

I decide to make an effort and descend
but they've locked the door from the inside again.
I'm too awkward to knock. "Excuse me, may I be let
out?" Or to ask why exactly we are locked
in at night, and apparently during the day as well.

In case of fire, we treasure the terrace keys.
we'd jump to the neighbor's terrace and
lower ourselves onto the adjacent stairs.

Grounding? When there is no horizon in
sight, I connect with the sky.
look up to the endless expanse and
exhale. Not, in fact, caged.

In case of emergency,
I will push off from
the terrace
and fly.

Landon

* * * * *

Contradiction Distance Hesitation Gender binary norms Food mixing Idealism Chador/burqua Good Corruption **Environmentalism** Power of music Reflection Change God Inertia Disparities **Familiarity** Comfort zone Caste system **Time** Gentrification Multidimensional life Socializing Communication Café Coffee Day "Make it matter" Knowledge Solitude **Home** Development Political economy Privilege Intersectionality Aversion to fixation on the uncomfortable Generosity **Someday** Group travel **Generosity** Home Language politics Unexpected passion Details Missing out Language **Exposure** Passivity Human body **Study Abroad** The awkward feeling when you've already tried to communicate 3 times and neither person has any clue what's going on and you realize you're never going to figure this out **Sensitivity** Returning home Oppression Representation Home Capitalism **Self discovery** Idea of using a play to create social change Cleanliness **Honesty** Self-determination Saying goodbye Study abroad Generosity Charity Meaning **Exposure** Going home **Authenticity** Love, personal responsibility and tradition **Good life** Direction that I've completely lost in this Bangalore smog Independence Moving forward **Home** Inspiration **Generosity** struggles Stepping up and stepping down The end **Activism** Unlearning Mediation Adjust-ment Helplessness Safety Homestay Farming **Helplessness** Suffering Feeling, exhaustion, stress, learning Returning home Love, personal responsibility and tradition Charity **Generosity** Human body Saying goodbye Passivity Study abroad Intersectionality Development Missing out Aversion to fixation on the uncomfortable The awkward feeling when you've already tried to communicate 3 times and neither person has any clue **IDEA**

Dear Home,

I walk a half hour alone to the restaurant and realize no one is staring at me. I sit alone in the European restaurant and realize no one is staring at me. Have I really never been alone here yet?

Maybe I've just gotten more comfortable with myself here. I'd been feeling so self-conscious that I could feel everyone around me. I don't feel so much like that now that a lot of the shock has worn off. There's more time to rest, smaller groups, and a lot of meetings near the host families . And honestly being sick has made me feel much more subdued.

I used to wonder a lot about what being home meant, and I imagined it as a place I would suddenly find myself in, where I made sense and felt comfortable and rooted. The more I travel, the more I realize how much America is my home. Even with all of its regional differences, to be almost anywhere in America seems like it would feel more intuitive than here.

Maybe it just takes going away to realize how "at home" you were in the first place, and that home is the things you stop seeing, like the place you live, the way you drive or look to cross a street or how you talk to someone at a grocery store. Perhaps that is more the meaning of home than how comfortable you are able to be within yourself. And that feeling of really finding yourself satisfied or at ease in the world is just a matter of finding yourself, your dreams, and your chosen family so that the world doesn't feel so random or distant.

Landon

* * * * *

Dear Study Abroad,

I am still trying to mull over and make concrete (is there a word for that?) why you are important to me. I am big on making action matter. Many of my friends have also studied abroad or spent time overseas — this, however, is my first time as a conscious adult. This stay in Bangalore has been expensive — and it means a lot that my mother (and my cousin!!) contributed so much, financially, to something she knew so little about (though I'm sure she would do anything for me, because she's my mommy and that's what mommies do). It's such a big risk, sending your child out into the world like that — so what does she get in return, if anything? What do I get in return? What do I earn? And how has this trip been important to me?

People who choose to study abroad often say it's "fun," it's a "good experience." People appreciate the experience as a résumé builder, and it's totally cool to have class in a different country, to fuck around in another country's locale (I mean that in the gentlest, most generous way possible — no offense or hard feelings intended) — and all of that is good and fun, but it isn't what I am looking for. I want both breadth and depth and meaning out of this experience because to really invest thousands of dollars into something like this — it's not just a walk in the park, or a joyride. I didn't want to learn something here that would've been equally viable in the U.S.

So why study abroad? (My reasons and other's reasons)
• To be in a new place (in order to...)
• To experience new sensations
• To get and feel lost, a feeling that isn't common anymore — because of technology (iPods, GPS, the internet)
• To "experience new cultures" (What does this actually mean?)
• To be submerged in a new culture, to be immersed in a new way of thinking/living
• To get outside of your comfort zone!!
• To explore other cities/countries

Why do I think studying abroad is important? Getting lost is an important feeling. It's terribly important to get out of your comfort zone and start pushing yourself often. To challenge yourself.

There are SO many people and places in this world. The city where you live, breathe, love, learn, work, exist... is just one small place, a niche. A literal hole in the wall, relative to the whole, wide world. You need to get out there while you still have the time and energy and opportunity to do so. How do others live? How do others interpret this world and what can you learn from them? What does beauty, happiness, despair, respect, love, affection look like here? Over there? What kinds of stories, dreams, hopes drive people here? Over there?

What do we learn about ourselves and others as we put our mind and bodies in different mental, emotional, and physical spaces?

What is global citizenship?

So what should I say when my friends, family, peers, students, supervisors, teachers ask: how was studying abroad?

What did you learn? How was this experience valuable? Why Bangalore?

I'm still trying to figure these things out... Maybe the answers are still out there...

Joanne

* * * * *

Dear Generosity,

You come in so many different forms for me. In general, you give me joy, comfort, satisfaction, or all of the above.

Today, I sat in the sun and stared up at the blue sky until the sun set. I acted on an impulse and got my ear pierced. I spoke my thoughts honestly in class and with Anu. Being generous to myself provided a reflective space for me to process my time here.

But, India has challenged me to find generosity in new ways. Am I being generous to think my dollars to rupees transactions are benefitting someone? Am I being generous when I play into a Mount Carmel College girl's idea of what it means to be American - the privilege and materialism? Sometimes, there's a fine line between generosity and honesty. I want to say it's a tiresome life to be in a huge city like Bangalore, but should I instead express admiration for the people who seem to thrive here? Similarly, there are times when honesty is far better than generosity. I don't feel the need to be generous about the trash or the noise pollution here, for example.

In turn, I'm negotiating ways to be generous with my perspective. It's not always fair to look through the lens of a privileged American woman or a Seattleite or a citizen of a country that is 167 years older than politically independent India. When is it ok to be sure of my opinion and my culture? When will I benefit most from keeping an open mind and momentarily letting go of my westernized lens? I really want to be generous but it is extremely difficult on a personal level. I believe, though, that the practice I'm getting here with being generous will help me back home. I'm looking forward to viewing my hometown and Seattle with more generous eyes.

Sincerely,
Annika

* * * * *

Dear Generosity,

Why is it that I must unlearn everything I have ever learned, to enact you? I was taught to be critical to ideas without recognizing that that, too, implied generosity. I was conditioned to be aggressive, to attack the world in order to understand it with greater depth, but why was that the case? How did it become easier for me to be generous with other human beings in interactions, yet be so unkind to myself and the ideas which fill my brain? In almost every context of learning—academic or otherwise—you are perceived as a weakness. Well, I write to you to resist that notion.

Generosity, you are forgiving to the flaws embedded in being. You allow for us to step back from a space of anger into one of understanding. You enable one to engage with problematic ideas, rather than dismiss them as such without moving beyond frustration. But, am I overly-idealizing you, generosity? Are there spaces in which it is okay for me to express genuine frustration? Well, yes—but that does not mean that you do not deserve a chance. I should indeed incorporate you into my every thought, word, and action but, the golden question is *how* do I do that when I've already been conditioned to engage with the world in a certain way? How do I balance genuine feelings of outrage, with you? What does the process of unlearning even look like? Recognizing that one has not been generous is but a first step, and I have already begun to negotiate my space to include you. I have recognized angst, quelled it, and replaced it with you. I have danced with you in my mind, despite the feelings of frustration in my heart. Nevertheless, I must try harder. When will I reach the point in my life when practicing you becomes as natural as inhaling and exhaling? When will you become so normalized that I no longer have to force you (or rather, find you deeeeeep inside)? Most of all, what will it take to share you with those around me so that they, too, can engage?

Generosity, you are too kind, and I will muster up the courage to be like you. I want to thank you for existing inside me, and I am aware now that my task in the coming weeks will be to unearth you from within. I look forward to it.

Warmly,
Margaret

* * * * *

Dear Sensitivity,

When Anu asked our class, "Did we have to come here to learn what we learned?" I almost had a panic attack. Why? Because this was my thought process in five seconds:

As a foreigner, I'm naturally more observant here. I am hyperaware. 1) A radio ad for "upper class homes" was done entirely in English and had a voice actor with a British accent. 2) I've only seen British literature (Shakespeare, Sherlock Holmes, etc...) on my host sister's bookshelves. 3) Whenever I talk to a native Bangalorean, 9 out of 10 times, they will mention pollution in the first 30 seconds. Details like these stay on my mind for days. It's almost like I've gained a sixth sense!

I'm not sensitive to my familiar environment. I've been desensitized to most problems of race, gender, class in the U.S. I thought back to my assignment in spring quarter. We picked a destination and wrote what it felt to be a tourist there. I toured a Sunday market in an upscale neighborhood. At the time, I thought it was a cute, pleasant tour. Then someone in class asked how many people of color were at the market. I said 2 or 3. Only then did I digest the unsettling information that in a city as diverse as Seattle, I only encountered 2 or 3 people of color on my trip.

Some details like these fly by me but even when I notice societal problems, I think, "At least it's better than Korea." Or "The political gridlock is an impossible barrier to pass." I don't want to play the blame game, but I've been raised to think that the U.S. is the best place to live in the world. I've been told countless times by my parents, cousins, uncles, and aunts that I am privileged to get to live in the U.S. My grandmother fled from North Korea during the war and grew up in the aftermath of it when the country had nothing. To this day, she always reminds me to thank my parents for bringing me to the U.S. In these ways, I have internalized the fact that I am privileged. I should be grateful. But how do I be thankful and critique at the same time? How do I de-desensitize myself?

Best,
Minjung Kim

* * * * *

Dear Exposure,

Throughout my month in India, I have been thinking about you a lot. It is not only exposure to a new country, but also to new sounds/sight/and smells that I never knew before. Although many of these new senses have been displeasing, you have made me a more critical person who is more aware of how the world works.

You have also demystified India for me, because I am realizing more and more that India is not so different from the U.S. as I once thought. It has been refreshing to be able to go to a live meat market to see how meat is prepared for consumption and ride in a rickshaw with the wind blowing in my face. In the U.S., we don't have to breathe in exhaust during traffic because we sit inside the car all day. In reality, traffic in the U.S. is just as bad or worse, and releases probably more exhaust into the atmosphere. We have factory farms that hold thousands more animals in worst conditions, while also polluting the water and air in those states.

One of the best parts was when you introduced me to the workers from the garment industry. I was surprised to find that these women want to work in the garment factories, and do not want factories to be shut down in their communities. They only want more protection and rights as workers. These women are housewives, garment factory workers, and activists. They don't complain about their situation, they fight. People in India have much greater obstacles in life that I would probably never experience in my lifetime, but they don't let these corrupt systems stop them from living or being happy. Through stepping outside of my comfort zone, you have showed me what it means to live simply and appreciate the small things in life.

Sincerely,
Vinnie

* * * * *

Dear Familiarity,

Over the past week, I feel like we've had a complicated relationship, and I've been able to see two sides of you in new ways.

You have been a huge comfort during this first week. Familiar bland foods are a welcome sight after so much spiciness. Restaurants with air conditioning and a clean atmosphere are a relief after walking on the street. High-end shopping malls bring to mind the comforts of home and the culture I have adopted for most of my life. I am grateful for these reminders, especially during moments of homesickness.

But I am also aware that there is another, more dangerous side of you, and my learning during this program has made it even more clear. I worry that as I become more familiar with this place and similar places, familiarity will turn into complacency. I am afraid that by becoming more integrated into these places, I will become less sensitive to the injustice that surrounds me. I know that this has happened many times in my life, even in America — a spark of indignation followed by slow recession into complacency. Perhaps it is because the truth of injustice is too painful to keep in my mind.

In any case, this is something for me to think about as I continue my studies both here and at home. Thank you for providing comfort during my travels, but please keep your distance in my struggle with social justice issues, if possible.

Nicole

* * * * *

Revolutionary movements have their own unassailable force, after all. People were astonished— young girls who had been considered meek and gentle turned overnight into tiger cubs.

—Antherjanam,
Cast me out if you will

Dear Activism,

    Learning about you in Bangalore has helped renew my own energy for activism. It's not that I had lost interest, but that I was feeling stuck. I was feeling stuck because in my own context, my activist communities are dominated by folks who are also stuck. We are stuck trying to name who is allowed to say what, and how, and in which spaces. I mean I love thinking critically about who occupies which roles in movements, but all this critique makes me feel like I am unable to actually facilitate social change. It seems like Environment Support Group (ESG) is really good at responding to the needs of communities. I wish I knew their trick to avoiding stuckness...I guess I just wanted you to know that I am ready to push myself to practice activism in a generous way.

                                  Best,
                                  Rukie

                * * * * *

Dear Good Life,

What is "A Good Life"? What does it take to be satisfied? I think being in a community where you both give and receive love is a part of a good life. Being financially stable, just enough to make sure you and your family have food, shelter, clothes, have access to healthcare and a good education, is another part. But it's rarely that simple. The money isn't always in the same place as your community, so which do you pick? Is there even an answer?

I guess the ideal would be to leave your community in search of jobs for long enough to make a set amount of money, then move back comfortable and secure financially. But how often can that happen? The community doesn't freeze while you're gone: people die, land develops, families move. What if when you come back, your community isn't the one you left, and you were too far away to have adapted with it?

Maybe my perspective is shaped by the consequences of a forced diaspora, so I can't understand the benefits of a chosen one. Maybe I'm speaking too generally and the specifics are different for each person and situation. My questions stem from one person I met, and his desire to move to the US temporarily. He wants a good job so he can prove to the girl he loves that she will be alright with him. He also wants a sense of security he doesn't feel now. There are no jobs for mechanical engineers in Bangalore so he's working in a call center, while studying to work in a bank, and — on top of that — attempting to open up his own call center out of his home. A mechanical engineering job in the US would be so much easier, and so much more profitable. But is it worth leaving his community? I'm not sure.

Sincerely,
Simon

* * * * *

Dear Generosity,

We talk about you a lot in class, and every week that we have been in Bangalore, I have experienced you in different ways. This week, my personal interactions taught me a lot about the ways that I can be generous to myself and others. You overwhelm me in the most positive ways – individuals this week reminded me that small gestures or acts of kindness make the biggest difference. Asima Auntie's friend from yoga invited us over to pooja and her son made an impression on me when he explained the significance of the tradition to me and my roommates. He expressed how excited his family was to share a bit of their culture with us, and said that they would keep us in their hearts. This opened my eyes to a whole new kind of generosity.

You manifest yourself in so many ways. I saw you this week when Asima Auntie threw me the most wonderful birthday party. I saw you yesterday when our rickshaw driver was eager to share his feelings with us about the infrastructure of the city, despite the language barrier. And I continue to see you every day when Anu and my classmates check in with me to see how I'm feeling. Generosity, you are about both showing people you care *and* sharing what you care about with others. Being in a new environment makes certain feelings and ideas more pronounced, and that explains why you look different to me every day based on the people I talk to. After each interaction this week, whether it was big or small, I gained a new understanding of you that I will hold in my heart and pass on to others.

Love,
Olivia

* * * * *

Dear Someday,

Someday I won't bother finding the perfect sentence to begin this letter but understand that it's the way you finish that matters. Someday I will be so passionate about an issue that those around me will feel the fire in my eyes, voice, and heart. Someday much of this will matter less and some of this will matter much more. Someday I won't stand idly by in the face of injustice and unfazed by blatant inequality. Someday I hope. Someday I will learn to express the confusion boiling inside me and escape the paralyzing weight of passivity that chains me to the floor. Someday I will mind my mind and voice my heart. Someday you'll see.

Someday I won't fear love, fear connecting to others, to open up, to empathize, to cry with you, to cry in front of you, the fear of run-on sentences. Someday my past will not govern my future. Someday I won't stand behind the defensive walls of humor and sarcasm afraid of being opposing or offensive. Someday this letter will serve as a physical reminder of a moment in my life when real change started to occur in my life. Someday writing won't be so difficult.

Someday I'll come back to India and sit out on this rooftop beneath the stars and listen to the sounds of the bustling city in the distance while the near howls of stray dogs guide my calm. Someday I'll find God in a book, a temple, in everything, in myself. Someday the sound of a palm tree blowing in the wind like rain kissing the ground will be proof enough of God or whatever we want to call it. Someday I pray. Someday will this under-utilized and at times underwhelming yet ceaseless sense of duty and 'want' prove worth anything at all? Someday will soon be today, so I have to work harder and care deeper; if we all do that then someday this world we live in will be a better place, right?... Won't it?

Chris

* * * * *

Dear Authenticity,

      Why do people feel the need to define you? You are every-where, but due to many preconceived notions you are invisible to many. To whom are you more important – the observer with the expectations, or the producer of the "authentic"? If an observer of "authenticity" is making decisions of what an "authentic" someone or something is, then the power dynamic is skewed because the "decider" has the power to define, but the "authentic" has the power to just exist on their own terms and rock the observer's worlds (if the observer is receptive to seeing this). It's so dismissive when people refuse to accept you in all your shades.

      It is American culture that provides a particular aesthetic and concept of what you are to us. You are exoticised and you must not resemble what we see in the U.S. Tell me, why is a poor person, or a hodgepodged home, or a lack of electricity more of an "authentic" representation of India? You are not supposed to be familiar – you are supposed to be humbling to us. When you show up at a mall or in lan-guage or in advertisements, we see ourselves and that doesn't make sense to us.

      To have these expectations of authenticity is to always be shielding our understanding. All experiences had, all feelings felt, all realities lived – they are all equally real, authentic and worth legitimizing. I feel like our constructed views of you are very, very hard for us to see, because why would we look at ourselves in order to see the "authentic India?" Other than self-referencing, of course...

You are so straightforward, yet so elusive.

Jenny

* * * * *

Dear Time,

You've managed to pass slowly and quickly here in Bangalore. Every day feels like a week and an hour at the same time, and I have one week left to make the most of you.

To be honest though, I feel tired and need more of you. I need more time to sleep, time to process, time with my host family, time on the toilet, time with our class, time for myself, time to write TIPS, time to digest food, time to play volleyball on the terrace with my host brothers, time to late night chat with Fabiola in our homestay, time to learn how to make lemon rice, french braid my hair, and navigate my way back to my host home without getting lost.

If there was time for all of this, my days would feel complete, but I'm settling for the time I do have. At least I'll have more of you back in Seattle, but you will certainly feel different from Bangalore time.

Yours truly,
Rukie

P.S. Sorry I didn't have time to write more.

* * * * *

Dear Helplessness,

Hearing about this work, all of these problems, I feel helpless. Looking out the bus window at the houses, highways, temples, trash, and farms makes me feel helpless. And not in the humbling small-ness of the stars, mountains, and seas kind of helpless. No, it is more of the rapidly rising water but I cannot swim helpless. I am learning about so many issues, hearing about so many sufferings, understand-ing so much inequality, only to realize I do not have the tools to mend even one tear in the fabric of society. What am I responsible for, if not for everything?!

This has not helped. This letter, this trip. They have only exacer-bated my clear inability to take action. Furthermore, who wants some white dude coming in and telling them how to "fix" their life? How much easier it is to pretend no one could use my help, that I have very little power, that the world is equal and fair. I am here. I see it is not so, not only in India, but also in Seattle. Yet I feel helpless nonethe-less. The only comfort is the rain. It hits my head the same way it hits someone else's. A woman. A man. An activist. A bystander. If only for a moment, we are all equally wet.

Marcello

* * * * *

Dear Contradiction,

I have been noticing you in many expected and unexpected places. The way you move in the lives of people is so fluid. What an amazing idea you are — I find your existence very interesting. I love that you exemplify how truth is not a static by showing how there are many (equally valid) opposing truths. Through you, I understand (just a little) better how you contribute to the beauty in peoples' lives (alongside the frustration and difficulties that people suffer). You, contradiction, are created by the very truths people experience. Truth is the very creator of contradiction through its own multiplicity.

Through our own dynamic lives, our truths also evolve and change. This makes the contradictions react in kind, changing and evolving. The constant motion and intersection of realities make the contradictions so jarring and disorienting on their own. But when I shift my perspective a tiny bit and see how a contradiction interacts with the truths and other contradictions, it suddenly makes so much sense why everything is often confusing and overwhelming.

I see that when I bother to notice your complexities I discover a secret code and I sense discovery. It's so much easier to get clarity about a contradiction once it's traced back to its roots. It is fascinating to "discover" these codes of contradiction, particularly when I open my eyes enough to recognize it in my own life and in my own actions, beliefs, and words.

It is also (apparently) much easier to see and understand contradictions if you "zoom out" your focus enough and become a bit removed. It seems silly to think I've gone to the other side of the world to look at my life in the U.S. but that is what is happening. And while it may sound silly, the contradicting truth is that it is easier to self-examine when you are removed from the familiar.

Jenny

* * * * *

Dear Environmentalism,

For the last several months I've stopped truly believing in you. I've felt sort of jaded about how people act about being green, like it's a ticket to moral superiority, looking down on those who are less green. I see it in the United States as a class symbol. The conversation is framed in a way that makes you feel you could never do enough because the world is dying.

Class yesterday made me feel like there is valuable work being done and that trying to conserve is worthwhile. It hit home to see the toxic landfill full of plastic bags, like, wow, these get in a truck and go to a landfill where they just sit for twenty years. It's not just about something intangible like global warming — it's not about the apocalypse, it's about water drying up and it's about people. It was really helpful to remember these things.

Bhargavi, Mallesh and all of the staff are so sweet and down to earth. We never hear them blaming problems on apathy or ignorance. In the U.S. it seems like the story goes "If only people would compost (or buy this product, or eat this diet), our world could be saved!" But wealthy communities tend to be the most actively green while the environmental impacts of toxic refuse are far greater in poorer communities.

Environment Support Group's (ESG) focus on the systemic issues such as the forces of money and business interests draws the focus away from individuals being good or bad. And I never get the sense that the amazing work they do makes them feel superior to others. This attitude of simply caring and wanting to do the work without it paying off some moral debt seems so natural to them. ESG took me away from the pettiness of the green social scene of Seattle, where environmentalism gets racist and classist and just plain elitist real fast. I think I can also get to a point where my actions are tied to what I want for the world without guilt, panic, or superiority.

Landon

* * * * *

66

Dear Self-Discovery,

All the corny shit I have been told for so long seems to be earning its keep in my mind. Self-Discovery, it seems you have been hidden in the deep recesses of my consciousness for years and years. I just had to turn over some stubborn rocks and embrace the words of those in my life to find you. That is not to say that I didn't know who I was before this trip; it's just that my ambitions and struggles didn't really match up with the way I have been morphing as a human being in the world. I am telling you this, Self- Discovery, to avoid the cliché concept that traveling has revealed all of myself....to me. It hasn't. I just see my place in the world differently.

We are all just people: struggling, laughing, crying, dying, eating, pooping, having sex, and listening to our favorite music. We are all just trying to live our lives the best we can. When a simple concept like this clicks in my head, my first reaction is to feel stupid that I hadn't understood it before. But once this frustration passes, my relationship with you, self-discovery, grows stronger. I get emotional and contemplative, and write in my journal because the thoughts in my head must get out. Another realization that connects to you, is my ambitions and future. I have wanted to dedicate my life to making a difference in the world. I still want to do that, but I see the value in taking pressure off myself to just live and see where my experiences take me. When it comes down to it, I can't make a difference if I am not feeling happy, healthy, and fulfilled. If I have learned anything from this experience in India, it is that I need to do what makes me happy when I have the time and passion to. Youth is not something to be wasted on planning out the rest of your life and worrying constantly about your test scores. I'm trying to find the middle ground and my journey to do so may take me to many different places.

Dear Self-Discovery, you have always seemed like such an abstract idea, but I am starting to make out the shapes and figures in your mess of lines and brushstrokes. I can't wait to see how I interact with the world back at home.

Love,
Amy

* * * * *

Dear Exposure,

It's funny how everything is hidden so "well" in America. We drive in air-tight cars and think there is little to no pollution in our cities unless we can physically see it. In our air-tight box cars, we cannot smell the smoke of the exhaust coming out of thousands of trucks and cars going 60+ MPH at any one point on the freeway.

We buy meat in packages at grocery stores and do not question its origin or the fact that it was a living being maybe a few weeks ago. We claim to live in a post-racial society because we celebrate Martin Luther King Jr Day every year and the Civil Rights movement has "already" happened. We throw our trash away only to never see it again or question where it goes.

American society has taught the average American citizen to mindlessly perform these daily tasks while the government ensures 'it will take care of the rest.' It is not until the raw moment you're in a rickshaw and have a cloud of coal black fuel exhaust blow in your face from the bus 5 feet in front of you do you wonder if India is just that much more polluted or if it's hidden so well from us in America in our air-tight box cars. It could possibly be 10 times worse but we would never know because of the non-existence of rickshaws or other similar modes of transportation in America.

You buy your meat fresh in Bangalore and often see your meat live right before the butcher cuts its head off and skins the rest of the animal before selling to you at the open meat markets. The buyer knows exactly what they are getting into and at what cost.

India attempts to cover and hide caste and the discrimination that comes with it with little success – it is something that can be identified from your name, where you go to school, where you live, what you eat, and what job you maintain. If someone cannot tell by these characteristics and feels the need to ask, the information is shared openly as fact.

As far as hiding trash goes, tell me why it took me a trip to India to show me the first landfill I've ever seen on earth even though I've been throwing trash away for over 20 years... I feel like this trip to a local landfill was long overdue and is something that every elementary school child should go to in order to be more conscious of the waste that individual will be producing for the rest of their life – imagine how much garbage we can save (by recycling or composting) with early education! The possibilities are endless.

To wrap up, while things in Bangalore may not all be perfectly sustainable, clean, and best for this earth, at least they're not pretending it is and it's all exposed. American society is probably one of the most sheltered societies that trusts in the government/higher powers to make the best decisions. Sometimes these 'best decisions' lead to a cover-up of the truth and misconceptions of the realities we live in.

Yuck,
Fabiola

* * * * *

Dear Home,

What are you? All my life I've imagined you as a place. When I was little I heard a story of how the Shah, before boarding his plane for exile, knelt down and took a handful of Iranian soil with him. So I guess I always thought that was the problem: I just wasn't on the right soil. But even in Iran I feel isolated. I don't know many people my age, I don't know a lot of the customs, I can barely read the language. So is it the soil?

One person I met wants to leave Bangalore and work in the US. He wants the money, the security, but mostly to escape caste. He thinks money will fix his problems—honestly it might—but at what cost? In the words of Junot Diaz, "what do you know about diaspora?" What do you know about isolation, racism, and living thousands of miles from your friends and family?

I know my dad still wants to go home. He brings up his friends and stories and smiles, like nothing material in this world can compare to his memories. Two and a half years ago when we went together to visit Kermanshah he was the happiest I had ever seen him, or have seen him since. I think he always planned to go back. But the revolution happened when he was in college and he had to stay. Then the recession happened and he had to push his retirement back a few more years. And the last year of instability in Iran has made any long term plan for living there almost impossible. So it gets pushed back. But every year added is another relative lost. First his grandparents (before I was born), then his aunts and uncles (I went to the funerals as a kid), and now his friends and cousins (people I grew up seeing on visits—people he grew up with). His parents are the only ones left of their generation, and they're 89 and 80.

I know it weighs heavily on him that he's not there with them. And I think he knows that he doesn't have many years before his entire community in Iran is gone. And when that time comes, I don't think the soil will do much to console him.

Simon

* * * * *

Dear Honesty,

I never trusted you. You've always gotten me into more trouble than you're worth. Maybe that is because you only ever come after intricate works of fiction? I'm employing you in my life now, like in our Theater of the Oppressed workshops. I hoped it would feel liberating. But it doesn't feel good. For once you've elicited positivity from others: "I'm so honored to hear your story!" "It was so inspiring!" "You're so brave!" This positivity from outside of me is no match for the negativity from within me. My dad used to say that if you weren't doing anything wrong you wouldn't be scared of the truth.

I worry that you make things too real. With you, the past isn't a story separated from me by time, distance, and state of mind, but it becomes me. Do I want that? What is at stake when I claim or disown my own stories? Are our stories even our own? Do I deserve my story? If it isn't a story anymore but has become me, what do I call what I have shared? Honesty, are you for me or for others? Do I or should I have expectations that come with my honesty?

When Deepak came to talk with us as part of a panel on art and activism put on by ESG for our class, one thing I got from his work was the ability to tease out a story with another story, like when he dressed up like a woman from mythology, performed her character in a public place, and was able to engage people in conversations about gender. Is this what I want my story/self-sharing to do? To make space for the stories/selves of others or to spark dialogue between the two stories/selves?

Ok Honesty, honestly I think, all this questioning aside, I think my story/self should matter, I don't know to whom, and yet I think my story/self doesn't matter . My story/self's personal history might "inspire," "create points of connection" or nurture sympathy, but at the end of the day no matter how I choose to use you, you are with me, you are always with me. I have continuously failed to lie to myself, I can't hide from you, even in Bangalore.

Sasha

* * * * *

People we have interacted with in Bangalore AT Mom Friend **Little girl looking at your mother looking at me looking at her daughter peeing in the street** Sasha my classmate Older white American man who dresses as Gandhi AT ESG's Leo ESG's Bhargavi Niece New friend from Mt. Carmel College Ambassadors **Man laying face down in the gutter** ABA Amy AT Saraswati Du Village leader from Chelakeri who organized a protest of 1000 people and 4000 sheep Street vendor Woman at Shivajinagar **3 beautiful girls** classmates in our program Beggar child Mr. Mallesh Mr. Mallesh Mamma in the village government school Friend **Sweet rickshaw driver** Ma'm AT Friend Mr. Sharat the civil engineer **AT** Family Schoolgirl asking extremely important and stumping questions Young woman from Mt. Carmel College Girl student from **Little beggar girl I saw near the Regional Institute for Cooperative Management** Mr. Mallesh's village AT All the mates on our program Mamma **Vendors in tourist markets** Host families Host sister Families living in the cement house on my homestay house street Mom Curious boys AT **Friend's father of our host brother who died in a scooter accident** Monkey sitting on our front porch Son of the lady we go to yoga with who invited us to pooja AT Friend Mommy Man getting attacked by the police Host **Girl I read about in the paper who was bitten by a snake and died** Auntie's daughter in law Dr. Thekur Friend Classmates on our program Homestay mother Desis **Saraswati Du** Garment factory workers **God** Guy who yells "hey!" outside out window everyday MECHA Shah Rukh Khan AT Badass women in India Friend Mr. Manoj the tailor Mr. Mohamed **White American Man Who Dresses as Gandhi** Anawallah the ISD operator at Mobility India Brother Sister Boy who lost **PERSON**

Dear Man Lying Face Down in the Gutter,

How can I help you? Forgive me for being a white savior, but I legitimately just want to help another human being.

I saw you when we were driving past with my host family. At first I wasn't sure what exactly I saw because it was dark and you didn't look like a human shape. Then I realized you didn't have arms. I wanted to cry. I pointed you out to my roommate in hushed tones. Deep down I knew we couldn't stop to do anything, but I wanted to think otherwise.

Dear man lying face down in the gutter, you're not the first person I have seen here with missing limbs. I remember my first time at the Shivajinagar Marketplace in Bangalore, a dusty, packed section of maze like streets, filled with people of all walks of life. There were beggars being wheeled down the streets on carts, some with acid burns on their faces, some with deformed hands and legs, and even those pulling themselves along the ground with what was left of their extremities. I felt fear and concern and confusion. I was not the only one. But for some reason, man lying in the gutter, seeing you alone, at night, not moving, in the dark, facedown, made all the difference for my reaction. After I saw you, I started tearing up and kept looking out the window not speaking.

My roommate whispered to me, "What could we have done anyway?" I had a few plans. Dragging you to the hospital, covering you with a blanket, getting you warm again. I may have been too idealistic, but that wasn't the point for me. I was trying to trust that humanity isn't a passive-aggressive bystander. But by doing nothing I felt like I proved that concept to be right.

I hope that you are alright, sincerely. I don't know what happened to you, but it's not fair and we both know it. I wish I could change things, but I don't know how. Forgive me for my privilege; I am just another person like you. I wish I could have helped you, from one human to another.

Love,
Amy

* * * * *

Dear Anu,

Unpacking and discussing the gender and violence conference on Saturday left me very emotional. I know, by now, I sound like a broken record — and by the time you read this, it's probably old news, but the issues our class brought up still resonate with me. I find it difficult to be generous when such a large part of me wants to call people out on their bullshit. I don't mind coming off rude, angry, or overly critical; I do mind that I sometimes step on people's toes and feelings in the process of trying to drive across what I think is an important point to make. I, however, am not always fully aware of the appropriate contexts to open certain conversations about possibly thorny issues. I sometimes "information vomit" or get off track or become unnecessarily focused on something trivial someone might have said in passing. I've upset people or derailed meaningful conversations because I've been unable to let go of things that probably should not have garnered the attention and anger that they drew out of me.

I have a big personality — and a big mouth. I learn through talking and I sometimes overtake conversations that should belong to someone else, or go in a direction that would be more fruitful if I could just shut up and listen for once. I'm trying to shut up and listen, but my heart feels so heavy and my head is always swimming. I feel like verbally vomiting half the time, and most of it is just mumbo jumbo until I have the time and space to process and organize everything.

I didn't want to degrade any of the panelists at the conference, because they're all human beings who are genuinely trying to do their own versions of "good work." I wasn't so generous at the conference. I made some pretty gnarly faces. I think I was confused for most of the time, and the rest, awestruck at how amazing Bhargavi was (and you, too!).

I brought up the conference not to dwell bitterly in the past, but because well after our group reflection session, something very tangential but heavy and confusing remained in my mind. Someone who is very dear to me was the victim of sexual assault when they were young. One of the panelists' story about his own daughter's assault, and his insistence that "men are clueless," triggered a train of thought in me that made me reconsider the idea of ally-ship more critically. I don't think he was doing anything morally wrong when he was trying to express what he thought was one way to better create a safe space for girls and women. He based it off his own experiences.

But how do men stand up for women's human rights without reproducing unequal power dynamics? Or the other way around?

As a feminist, I've been taught so much of the history of women's oppression (often perpetuated by a small group of powerful men and patriarchy), that when I consider, also, the human rights of men — I become reflexively defensive.

How do I, as a feminist, speak for the rights and empowerment of women while also juggling a respectable space for men who also experience the troubles imposed by patriarchy? How do we build this ally-ship while also maintaining each of our very separate, different, but connected identities?

Joanne

* * * * *

Dear Ms. Saraswati Du, the Dalit activist who came in and talked to our class on August 22, 2013,

My name is Rasan Cherala. I am 19 years old and I was born in the U.S. and moved to India at the age of 5. I "lived" in India for 7 years. Today, I realized that the India I lived in is much different than the India I see around me now. In my time here, caste seemed like an obsolete system, simply something that operated in an era long gone. Never would I have thought that caste could affect me in a way that could have long-lasting impacts. Although my parents both grew up in lower middle class families, they both came from Brahmin families. Did that give them a leg up in getting to the US? I think so. Their parents were educated and my parents' education was always first above all else. I do not think that their parents would have had the same kind of opportunities for education in a Dalit community. Larger structural forces proscribed and dictated that in a Dalit family or community, one could not get an education. My great grandparents were either teachers or farmers, or both.

You can't choose your family, where you're born, or the kind of life you are born into. However, you can choose to do something with the life you are given. It is one's drive and determination that helps one overcome insurmountable obstacles. Today, you showed me what it takes to overcome such obstacles of caste, class, gender, and social pressure. Today, you showed me the indomitable human spirit that even in the face of adversity, struggles on. You gave me hope because of your openness and kindness, and the way you said what you did. You looked me in the eye during the discussion and talked directly to me. You had no reason to do so.

Why should you have to talk to me, a high caste Brahmin from the US with incredible privilege? It's because you believed we could connect. After all, caste, race, creed, they're all just social inventions used to oppress people. Like you said, we are all part of the human race. We all have a body, a mind, and feelings. We are not all the same, and we come to the table with differences — privilege, background, ideas. There should be more room for discourse. You were willing to step halfway to connect with me and I am more than willing to step all the way to connect as well.

I have been struggling to stay present because there has been so much going on in my life. But you made me feel like there was a need to stay present. There's more at stake than just my personal problems. I can take steps to break down barriers, to lead the way to a better situation where everyone is treated well. There is a better way, and each of us is a part of the puzzle. Change is the only constant, and perhaps my actions can help nudge those puzzle pieces into place, to make a better future. Thank you for coming in and helping me realize what I can do. You explained yourself when you didn't have to, and that helped me understand what you have had to go through. The fight for what you want goes on forever, against all odds, and though at times you may lose hope, you should never give up.

Sincerely,
Rasan

* * * * *

Dear Sweet Rickshaw Driver,

You are one of the good ones.
When I needed a ride and was worried about traveling alone, you were there.
You understood my heavy American pronunciation of my destination.
You agreed immediately to the meter price without taking advantage of my ignorance.
You drove quickly, but without taking unnecessary risks.
You knew the route and went straight there.
You helped me find change and never suggested I just pay extra.
You dropped me off safely at my destination.

So, thanks for a great experience. You are an honest guy making an honest living. I wonder, if all Rickshaw drivers were like you, would it be deemed safe for women to go out alone at night? Would that be enough? What is it exactly that makes women afraid? Is it family's warnings, dangerous men, or fear of the unknown?

If there were more eyes on the street, like yours, would the streets be safer? Or are gender biases so institutionalized that a few good people would not make much difference? Is the fear protecting the women or the oppressive system?

Could it be that my own fear is actually unfounded? Do I really need the protective male gaze over my life in order to be safe? Is the danger mostly in my head?

It's hard to say, because the truth is that awful things do happen. Women are often the targets of violence, harassment, looks, and uneven expectations. So, where does that leave us? What can we do?

I can discuss gender, and hear from garment worker unions and volunteer with groups like HHS (Hengasara Hakkina Sangha). But that doesn't feel like enough. I can recognize my own gender prejudice and assumptions and try to confront them while sharing my thoughts with others. But, there has to be more.

Kelli

* * * * *

To the friend's father of our host brother, who died in a scooter accident,

In India, it is difficult to forget that the interconnectedness of our lives is an intricate web of action and consequence. When so many people come together in a place such as Bangalore, it is nearly impossible not to see the variety and vibrancy of life here. Sometimes in Seattle, it is difficult to keep hold of the realities of other people's lives. It is easy to isolate myself, and get lost in my own thoughts, problems, and commitments. There, I can do that, but here I can't because so many people are visibly worse off than I am.

Life can take a turn suddenly - like my cousin's scooter falling sideways into a pothole, losing balance and somehow, seemingly magically, correcting itself. Sometimes, it feels like there is no rational explanation and death is one of those things. Death is difficult to rationalize because what comes next is unknown. We can debate about what comes next, or if anything comes next, but it won't make a difference to our loved ones who are dead and gone. Death is the great equalizer. It takes all, and spares no one. The richest of the rich and the poorest of the poor all face the same eventual fate. The difference is in how I decide to get there.

One of these days, my heart will slow and play its final beat. One of these days, my heart will stop, and the ground will collapse beneath my feet. These past few months, so many people I know have been close to death, or have died... What do I leave behind when I die? What will happen once my body has been turned to ash? What's important is that the legacy I leave behind be one I can take pride in. It's not just one action that leads to this, but, an action in the right direction is better than none at all, and is a good first step.

I can imagine the scene you faced. A woman on a scooter driving behind you is getting closer. She swerves to avoid a pothole. You continue your slow hobble, onward, forward, towards a future and towards your family. The scooter collides with you. You hear the crunch, and you're thrown onto the concrete road. The pain – as you fall to the ground trying to support yourself – is unbearable.

In India everyone goes where they need to go and does whatever they need to do. Most of the time, it works out and everyone gets home. For some of the people out there, they get hurt in the process. Unfortunately, you were one of those few. If you were a few feet farther back, maybe you could have avoided the internal bleeding – the mixing of cerebrospinal fluid and blood. Maybe if the lady on the scooter had turned around and stopped to make sure you were okay, you may still be here and I could be talking to you instead of writing about you.

But really, the problem was not you or the lady driving the scooter. You are both part of a system that perpetuates bribery, corruption, the take-it-easy, someone-else-will-take-care-of-the-problem attitude that pervades Indian society. Perhaps you would still be around if the contracting company that created the roads in the first place didn't have to bribe officials for permits, for jobs, and for taking shortcuts. If the government had built lights like it is supposed to on the streets, the woman on the scooter may have spotted you. Shit doesn't just happen. For every action there is a consequence.

There are people who make it happen and this leads to problems everywhere in India and the world. It doesn't affect the people in power making the decision. It affects those who are vulnerable and further down the line. It affects those people who are seen as unimportant. One of those people just so happened to be you. For that, I am sorry. I am sorry that no one has had the courage to stand up and say, "I will not pay the bribe to the police officer," sorry for none of us stepping up and speaking out against injustice.

Who knows what could happen tomorrow...people like you are affected like this every day. It just so happened that I heard about you. I didn't know you, but this is a salute to you. I don't want you to be forgotten. This letter is to a person who lived a life filled with responsibility and commitment, love, and faith. This letter is for you and those like you, who suffered from our collective inaction. I hope the end for you was not too painful, and that the love of your friends and family was evident in their presence. Perhaps you were embraced by either darkness or light.

Wherever you may have gone and whatever might have happened, I hope that your legacy is one that you would be proud of. Rest in peace, good sir. You left this world far too early.

Sincerely,
Rasan

* * * * *

Dear Girl I read about in the paper who was bitten by a snake and died,

I cannot stop thinking about you. You lived your short life in a cement block on a construction site while one or both of your parents toiled away, building a rich man's home. You died from such an exotic cause that it's difficult for me to even *fathom* your short life. And I'm constantly reminded of you because three small kids live the life you lived right across the street from me.

This morning as I waited for a rickshaw, I spotted those kids and they began a "dance-off" with us. It was a moment of pure joy for them and us – I hope you had moments like that, too. :)

There's another detail of your death that I keep thinking about. Your parents waited one full day before bringing you to the hospital. This can happen anywhere, but I realized the various factors that could have prevented your parents from treating you sooner. Just like the women who tirelessly work in garment factories, your parents probably thought a full day's paid work was too much to lose. Is it because of the immense pressure to keep up with Bangalore's globalization that young people like you fall by the wayside? It sometimes seems that you and other children living in poverty are neglected by society because your parents suffer years of stagnant wages and endless work catering to people with power.

Or maybe...a bored snake just simply decided to sleep where you were that day. Maybe your sad death is just another proof of how nature is more powerful than man. As humans, we all have so little control over what nature deals us – floods, impending water scarcity, unpredicted earthquakes. I didn't know you; I shouldn't care so much about what happened to you. I do hope, though, that your story stays with me and remains a small example of how forces much bigger than the individual are always present.

Sincerely,
Annika

* * * * *

Dear God,

I kind of feel sorry for you sometimes. I know that is probably not the proper language or wording to talk to you with, but what I mean is: for centuries other people (mainly men) have been putting words in your mouth, claiming them as 'words from God himself.' They basically take advantage of you and your name to shape their own respective societies and create myths and stories to scare people into living their livelihoods the way they wanted, to control them on how they live and move through life. It really causes me to question whether these manipulating people actually have faith and believe in you or are just doing it for personal gain. I strongly believe the latter.

When I first saw the government building (or should I say palace) in Bangalore, I was disgusted and confused by the huge statement written big and bold on the front of the building – "Government's work is God's work." I'm not sure if it bothered me so much that the government claimed to be as powerful as you, or if I was bothered by their strategy to continue to cause religious people never to question the work of the government or what, but it tore some strings inside me and made it impossible for me to ignore. It kind of reminded me of a line in a book I'm reading – The Uncomfortable Dead – talking about how Bush threw God out in his speeches whenever he could – "George Walker... appears to be honestly convinced that he and God (in that order) make up an impressive team." This just goes to show that whether in Bangalore, the US, or anywhere else around the world, people (particularly governments) are taking advantage of your name in order to control and continue to oppress their "followers."

There's a REALLY thought-provoking perspective that the novel gave concerning how the government's relationship with you is abusive, and the geographical layer of oppression that segregates "good" from "bad" and governments from citizens.

The Bad and the Evil according to La Chapis – The Uncomfortable Dead –

"The problem with the Bad and the Evil is geographical. The geography of evil was turned around, set upside down. So when they tell the story of creation, the rich turn everything around. According to them, heaven, or God, goodness, is up in the heights, while the Bad and the Evil, the Devil, are down below. But it really isn't like that. God is not up in the heights. To correct that mistake, God sent his son, Christ, to earth – to prove that goodness, heaven, is not up in the heights, far from what happens on earth.

The powerful of those times convinced everyone that the Earth was organized like heaven, that the Good were up high, the rulers, the ones in charge, and down under were those who obeyed, the Bad. So heaven was equivalent to the government, and God was equivalent to the ruler. And that's the way they used to justify, and continue to justify, the dictate that you have to obey the rulers. So you get Bush, who drags God up whenever he feels like it – he uses God to justify his every wrongdoing. Christ was crucified, because he came to question all this. And him being the Son of God, instead of meeting with the rulers, dining in their palaces, organizing a political party, and becoming their advisor, what did he do? Well, he went and got born in a manger, surrounded by animals; he grew up in a carpenter's shop and created an organization with the poorest of the poor.

Now then, would God go where Evil is? Of course not. He stayed with those at the bottom, and this tells us that goodness is not up in the heights – he would have been born in the home of that bastard Salinas de Gortari or that damned Bill Gates, but he wasn't. So heaven is not up there and neither is goodness. Evil is up there, on the right, with the rich, with those who govern badly, with the oppressors of the people. So where is goodness? We don't know. We'll have to find it.

I don't know, maybe goodness is down on the left, it might be the best place to start looking. That's why I look down when I pray; I'm praying to God, who is with the underdog. That's why I don't agree with the damn bishops and priests who are always siding with the rich and then becoming just like them, even in the way they dress..."

La Chapis (the character in the novel who is speaking) brings up some very interesting observations about the hierarchical geography of power, which makes me question why this observation is not more explicitly exposed (even though it's sitting right in front of our faces) to the general public. My assumption is that because it is those who remain in power that have the knowledge and teach the "others," the "followers," us "down below," never to question their actions and to remain obedient. I think more people need to start questioning. There is no such thing as civil disobedience when we are only fighting to get back what is rightfully ours – power. Let's not get me started...

Power to the people,
Fabiola

* * * * *

Reference and citations to novel:
Marcos, Subcomandante, and Paco Ignacio Taibo. *The Uncomfortable Dead: (What's Missing Is Missing): A Novel by Four Hands*. New York: Akashic, 2006. Print.

Dear three beautiful girls,

You might not remember me, but I remember you. I met you outside of your school after I was shown around. You were standing next to a group of boys who were getting all the attention from my group. When I noticed you looking in my direction, I smiled. You smiled back, so I walked over. Then we just looked at each other.

I don't speak your language, so I just did what the others were doing; I took your photo and showed it to you. You laughed and I waved goodbye.

As I walked away, my friend Marcello came up beside me. Thinking about our brief encounter, I mentioned that I wish I could have spoken to you. "What would you say?" he asked. "I would tell them hello. You are beautiful... After that I guess I'm not sure." I asked what he would say, and with a smile he replied, "Nothing."

And so, I've been thinking about our interaction. What is it that makes me feel like I need to say something to you? Is it my colonized mind that thinks you need my help? Is it my position of privilege as a wealthy, educated, white person? Could it be my age as an older woman? Was I looking at you three as sisters or as charity? Did I want to speak to you for your benefit or mine?

I have no idea. I don't even know what I would say to you. "Jesus loves you?" That would be confusing in this hurried context. "You can be anything that you want to be?" What right do I have to say that? Even telling you that "you're beautiful," seems to rely on my status as a white American.

But the truth is, I do have some power in this relationship. So right or wrong, my words might hold some weight with you. Do I have the right to use that power, though? Should I? I would use it with the best motives, but is that enough? Or maybe I'm overthinking it. Maybe I'm just another foreigner to you, and our interaction didn't mean a thing. In that case, even learning your language and saying the "perfect" thing wouldn't make a difference.

Maybe a smile is enough. Like Marcello said, maybe it's best just to say nothing. Maybe it's most powerful to just make eye contact, and smile, and share a moment of humanity. Maybe that is actually the most powerful thing that can be done for both of us. Maybe in that silent interaction, we each have the power to say something words can't.

Regardless, thank you for letting me step into your life. My name is Kelli. Nice to meet you.

Kelli

* * * * *

Dear little beggar girl I saw near the Regional Institute for Cooperative Management,

I saw you see me, Kelli, and Olivia. I noticed you immediately move toward us and you had a determined look on your face. You were probably only four or five years old. A busy street-side probably isn't where you should be. Seeing you like that was rather disheartening. Where were your parents? Did they care, or had they abandoned you? You were so scrawny, your greyish dress frayed at the bottom. The way you looked at us with hungry eyes was quite desperate. I didn't make eye contact with you but I wish I could have picked you up and played with you. You were adorable. Your tiny hands came and clawed at my jeans; and I looked away. There was nothing I could do.

After moving away from me, you went to Olivia and grabbed at her hand. Liv gave me a look of hopelessness. It's a look that I can't forget - one where she felt lost. She was confused and wanted to help, but didn't know how. Kelli also looked toward me, with a look that asked me what she should do. In that moment, I was just as lost as she was. Every time I see a beggar on the street, I'm reminded of you, little girl. The hunger in your wide, open, brown eyes is what I see in all of them. A hunger - for life, love, and the basic necessities needed to live. Know that there is someone out there who cares. Though I may have been unable to do anything then, maybe there is something I can do in the future. I hope that the tides of fate and the seas of time work in your favor. Though sometimes life can feel like waves pulling you out to open sea, you have to fight to live, to survive. I hope that somehow you get out of the situation you are in. I hope someone will be kind to you. Until the next time we meet...

Sincerely,
Rasan

* * * * *

Dear Vendors

     Why do you allow me to pay less than your initial offer? I love it when you tell me about your life, but my Western-ingrained values get annoyed when you only tell me about your struggles and strife. I get that pity usually works on the western value system, but I just think that you perpetuate the paternalistic, pity-centric dynamic that westerners have with foreign struggles of poverty. I also see how I play into these stereotypes, and I wonder how we can interact that doesn't reinforce the myths we have of each other while still getting you fair prices from us tourists.

Jenny

* * * * *

Dear Older American White Man Who Dresses as Gandhi,

I cannot even begin to understand you. I just can't.

I'll start by saying that I acknowledge my lack of information about you, your history, struggles, fears, loves, beliefs, and experiences. I know that this is a serious disadvantage in my ability to write you a letter, but I have too much to say and ask you to let this stop me.

But here you sit, placed amongst a group of women at a conference regarding violence against women. You are the only man. And you are dressed in a white sheet of some sort, with glasses, and sandals. I have a lot of questions to ask you.

First of all, why are you dressed like Gandhi? I have never seen this one before. Is this socially acceptable for a white man to do? What caused you to do this? Have you encountered backlash to this?

Once you have answered these questions, I would like to discuss the thoughts behind your comments (which you say you knew would make some people angry). Do you really believe that rape culture can be changed by the instruction of women? In response to this statement, I stood up in front of a room filled with people I did not know (well 25 that I did), and directed a comment at you. "How is it fair to excuse men for their actions because they are clueless? How do you think most women would take your comment that dual responsibility is assigned to women to instruct men and deal with the impacts men have on their accessibility to the social sphere?" I personally was very offended and fired up by this seemingly ignorant and simple-minded idea.

I know you were the only man on the panel, but that doesn't give you an excuse to blame dynamics of the conference on an imbalance. Given, the group of people on stage was somewhat thrown together, especially the American students. They basically just stood up there and gave all these young Indian women a lecture on the meaning of the term "rape culture." Despite all this, I wish they had chosen someone besides you. Your attitude, embracing the passive and peaceful protest idea to apply to this complex and active fight for equality and safety, just seemed plain ridiculous.

I don't plan on turning the other cheek. I'm the kind of girl who hits back.

Sincerely,
Amy

* * * * *

Dear little girl, looking at your mother, looking at me, looking at her daughter peeing in the alleyway,

When you have to go you have to go I suppose. I hope you know that I don't judge you for peeing in public, in fact you might not have given it a second thought. Well, I apologize for my naiveté, you might have felt secure under the watchful eye of your mother whereas I was so clearly lost and out of place. How did I find myself in that dimly lit alleyway in the middle of Bangalore, India?! What am I doing here? I guess I forget about the simple privileges I possess, especially in matters as basic as pee and poo. Privilege... I can *hold* it and forget it. You took my Indian public urination virginity and I won't forget that.

Chris

* * * * *

Letter to Minjung Letter to Rukie Letter to Bianca Letter to Vinnie Letter to Annika Letter to Marie Letter to Sasha **Letter to Olivia** Letter to Rebekah Letter to Divya Letter to Amy Letter to Simon Letter to Chris Letter to Margaret Letter to Kelli Letter to Fabiola Letter to Rasan Letter to Landon Letter to Jenny Letter to Joanne Letter to Nicole Letter to Marcello Letter to Rukie Letter to Minjung Letter to Bianca Letter to Vinnie **Letter to Annika** Letter to Marie Letter to Margaret Letter to Olivia Letter to Rebekah Letter to Divya Letter to Amy Letter to Simon Letter to Kelli Letter to Fabiola Letter to Rasan Letter to Landon Letter to Jenny Letter to Joanne Letter to Nicole Letter to Marcello Letter to Sasha Letter to Minjung **Letter to Rukie** Letter to Divya Letter to Vinnie Letter to Marie Letter to Sasha Letter to Olivia Letter to Rebekah **Letter to Bianca** Letter to Amy Letter to Simon Letter to Chris Letter to Margaret Letter to Kelli Letter to Fabiola Letter to Rasan Letter to Landon Letter to Jenny Letter to Joanne Letter to Marcello **Letter to Nicole** Letter to Minjung Letter to Rukie Letter to Bianca Letter to Vinnie Letter to Annika Letter to Marie Letter to Sasha Letter to Olivia **Letter to Divya** Letter to Rebekah Letter to Simon Letter to Chris Letter to Margaret Letter to Kelli Letter to Fabiola Letter to Rasan Letter to Landon Letter to Jenny Letter to Joanne Letter to Nicole Letter to Marcello Letter to Amy Letter to Chris **Letter to Margaret** Letter to Kelli Letter to Fabiola Letter to Rasan Letter to Landon Letter to Jenny Letter to Joanne Letter to Nicole Letter to Marcello Letter to Rukie Letter to Minjung Letter to Rukie Letter to Bianca Letter to Vinnie Letter to Annika Letter to Marie **Letter to Sasha** Letter to Olivia Letter to Rebekah Letter to Divya Letter to **SELF**

Dear Self,

What really hit me this week was the parallel between white privilege and Brahmin privilege. To the eye, Brahmins aren't as recognizable as white people. But, in certain situations, one can guess that a large part of the crowd is upper caste.

In America, because I've been discriminated against by the majority race, I was very aware of white privilege and how I was treated differently than a white person. I couldn't believe my white friends didn't realize this. But here in India... I carry so much privilege, it's crazy. I'm relatively fair, Brahmin, upper-middle class, American, English-speaking, and educated. If I were a man, I'd be the epitome of privilege in India. But I've been walking around without a clue. Over the last four weeks, I've slowly started to realize this. My father's family is not wealthy and my father worked hard to come to America, but the mere fact that he made it to the US probably reflects the privilege he's had as a Brahmin.

I didn't grow up thinking about caste, especially since my parents are an inter-caste love marriage. However, Ms. Saraswati Du told me I should start being aware of the space I take up, especially in India. I'm not going to beat myself up about the caste I've been born, nor can I just ignore my background (much like how people think that ignoring/denying racism is beneficial). I have no idea, though, how to think about my privilege, especially when it doesn't affect my life in America on an everyday basis. I'm totally confused, gah! It was a great last class day but I'm left with sooo many questions.

<3 Divya

* * * * *

Dear Self,

Where has the last week gone? I feel like just yesterday I arrived and was overwhelmed by so many contradicting emotions....

Discouragement and Inspiration. Discouragement when I saw people begging on the street and wanted to give them so much more than a biscuit. Inspiration when Ms. Bhargavi and Mr. Mallesh told us about the incredible accomplishments of Environment Support Group, and the fact that sometimes they need to be disturbed in order to work hard to solve social justice issues in their community.

Homesickness and Comfort. I miss my family and friends every day, and at the same time, everyone who is a part of this program makes me feel right at home.

I don't think I would have completely understood the contradictions we discuss in class until I experienced my own emotional contradictions, and that makes me feel extremely grateful to be here.

My head is still spinning, but with different thoughts. Especially after today's class. Our discussions about migration and community put a lot of things in perspective for me. Reflecting on our visit to rural Karnataka was important for me. While we were there, I experienced immense amounts of kindness from the local residents, and joy from Mr. Mallesh. The residents' kindness was incredibly welcoming and Mr. Mallesh's joy was contagious.

Today we went deeper than our initial observations from the village, and talked about how this visit can be related back to many stories of migration that we read in the spring. I enjoyed reading the stories, but nothing compares to witnessing someone returning to their home and thinking about what it means for them. I am so grateful that Mr. Mallesh shared his village with us. Our conversation today about what it meant for him to take us there put our visit in perspective.

I entered a community when I went there last weekend, but I am also part of different communities at home. Different parts of my idenity are linked with the communities I am a part of. How are these parts of my identity playing out or intersecting with the communities I visit elsewhere? Although my thoughts may not be fully formed, I am constantly being challenged to think about my identity and communities in different ways. When I travel in the future, this will always be on my mind.

Love,
Olivia

* * * * *

Dear Nicole,

I know it's been a rough week for you, health-wise, but I want to make sure you set aside time to think about some issues that have come up.

I think the most important issue for you to think about is the politics of photography. You have been one of the most avid photographers during this trip, and I think it would be valuable for you to devote some time to considering the discussions we had during our trip to Mr. Mallesh's village and the temples in Belur and Halebid. See, for instance, this photo you took of four strong women workers. Why did you snap this photo when you did?

Some questions for you to think about:

What is your role/purpose here in Bangalore?
What are the differences between taking pictures of people in our group and taking pictures of people outside of our group? Is there a difference?
How is the act of capturing a picture detrimental to the subject? The photographer?
How is the act of capturing a picture beneficial to the subject? The photographer?

How does one represent others responsibly in photographs?
Is this even possible?
How does one go about sharing the experience with those
back home? Are pictures helpful/harmful in this interaction?

This will be a long discussion. I'm sure you've realized by now
that none of our ideas/actions are as simple as you originally thought.
Luckily, you have an amazing group of classmates who are willing to
explore this with you deeply and generously. I hope you take advantage of this and take the opportunity to explore new ways of thinking.

Nicole

* * * * *

Dear Bianca,

After our lecture on development, its various connotations, and its manifestations, Kelli asked what you think Bangalore should do. You responded with, "Stop developing." Divya got offended about your response for a valid reason and said, "That's not fair, how can you say that you don't think someone should have the same things that you do, and because you don't think that they should?" You bit your tongue, because she was right.

How do you justify coercing people to believe and think the same things you do? How do you tell somebody that what they want is wrong? Everyone here aspires to have a middle class lifestyle, if not more. You see those who become distracted with material manifestations that represent ownership and possession, as if those arbitrarily measure happiness. At home you see how perverse that can be, because of the complacency that comes along with those privileges. But how can I blame them for wanting more, simply, just better. There are so many advantages in the US that I'm able to benefit from, so why shouldn't others be able to do the same?

Bianca

* * * * *

Dear Rukie,

    I am very sleepy/tired right now, and in a way, happy to go home, though I know I will miss our Bangalore community. In all of the contexts in which I've traveled, I've created meaningful relationships that I hold very dearly. And I have complicated feelings about travel -- what it means to come and go for pleasure, how to be an ethical tourist, trying to minimize my carbon footprint, etc. — Is it wrong to prioritize my desire to build relationships with people living elsewhere in the world over these complicated feelings? I know there is rapid connection via internet, but there is something very moving (both physically and mentally) about in-person contact and communication...It will be interesting to see what kind of connections I can keep.

Love,
Rukie

* * * * *

Dear Margaret,

The first week in Bangalore, you broke down in disillusion-ment. You felt your oozing privilege drip from your pores and flow through your veins. Becoming hyperaware of your privilege caused you to simultaneously feel, shame for having so much of it as well as, develop a sense of urgency not to waste your share.

Over the past four weeks, you have grown to understand that some positionality in the world is unchangeable. It is not fated, but ingrained, and rather than focusing on guilt associated with any privi-lege or shame over not having any other, you have learned to use your power to do some good. You had to (re)discover this by moving to ac-cept your being – but have you found that space yet, Mags? Have you learned to be okay with yourself in the world? I don't ask you these questions because I think being okay with yourself is an excuse to stop radically transforming. It is not. I ask you these questions because I know that a mind that is at peace can go so much further.

Keep stepping, because you have so much already. To stop now would be tragic.

Thank you,
Margaret

* * * * *

Dear Self,

It is ok to be ok. You know well enough that grief and sadness doesn't go away especially for someone so emotionally oriented and tends to want to experience emotions to their most radical depth. You've been told to not think so much, not to get so engrossed in critique and what is problematic, and to allow yourself to experience multiple emotions at once. Maybe all of this is connected?

It is ok to trust. When Anu asked us to organize some dancing on the bus, you were kind of gloomy, jealous of Mr. Mallesh's home and his joy in sharing his village with us. You weren't really readily equipped in that moment to be silly and social, but two things made us do it: 1) the thought "just do it" and 2) Anu being Anu. She doesn't ask much from us, so when she does ask something of me, I really, really, really, REALLY want to make it happen. Plus, I really, really, really, REALLY trust her. Her spontaneous requests/suggestions are always out of my comfort zone, but my respect, curiosity, amazement, and trust in her allow me to somehow override my overactive thoughts and I just do it.

In this "just do it" mode, I can set aside current feeling to make room for different kinds of emotional energy. It is also really fun: 1) the party on the bus was the most fun I have ever had, 2) there is a rush to doing what feels good without excessive mental work, 3) it is great to be able to exchange very positive feelings and energies, and 4) to be able to set grief and sadness aside for a little while, know that it will be there for me to experience in all of its depth and complexities later, and to add joy to whatever is happening for a little while. Feeling joy doesn't diminish your grief or sadness.

In the same way we think of gender being fluid and flowing, maybe emotions can be fluid and flowing. Maybe like us being genderqueer but with our emotions? I think the dance party on the bus was an example of how not thinking too much and allowing yourself to experience multiple emotions at once can feel viscerally. And it felt good, so let's try it again sometime.

Love,
Sasha

* * * * *

Dear Annika,

Remember the time you've spent alone, reflecting. Recently, you've realized the value and necessity of devoting time to yourself. This has given you a chance to find out how this trip is changing you.

Finally, you have started to *really* feel almost every sensation. I think part of your initial culture shock was a sensory overload, and it prevented you from recognizing distinct smells, tastes, sensations. Now, the smoothness of curd, the jolty rickshaw ride, and the rotting stench of trash heaps are becoming part of every day's rhythm. The sharp pang of missing family and friends is disappearing, being replaced with attitudes and emotions directed towards classmates. Finally, FINALLY, you feel *present*.

Now, can you pay attention to your body? Not just for health's sake, but also to observe the space you take up. How much space do you and your belongings occupy on a Bangalore street and in your homestay? I hope you return to the US more aware of your place in the world than when you came to India. This sounds big, but think of it in a small way. If you see your tiny place in the grand scheme of things, I think you can better contextualize ideas and issues without your background or your experiences clouding your judgments. Be a 'storywallah.' Become part of the network of humans crossing paths, sharing space, and inhabiting each other's lives in meaningful ways. This is the sign of a true global citizen.

Love,
Annika

* * * * *

MEET THE LETTERWALLAHS

AMY HERSH

Amy grew up in Marin County, California, where she fostered an early love for the environment, law, and justice. Amy moved to Seattle in 2010 to start school at the University of Washington, studying Environmental Studies and Human Rights. While at the UW, Amy has participated in the Mock Trial program, interned for several successful environmental organizations, and had the amazing opportunity to travel to India in the summer of 2013 with Dr Anu Taranath and 23 other classmates. Amy hopes to continue traveling and get involved in environmental movements around the world.

ANNIKA VAN GILDER

Annika is a sophomore at the University of Washington majoring in medical anthropology and global health. If she's not reading or writing for school, she'd like to be hiking in the Pacific Northwest mountains or dreaming up her next trip abroad. She is part of a grassroots movement to advance global health policy with the non-profit, Partners in Health, where she aspires to work one day.

BIANCA YOUNG

Bianca studies Geography, focused around globalization, development and healthcare. She envisages our space on the map in relation to the spaces of others.

CHRIS YOON

Chris loves to refer to himself in the third person. Though he has no idea what's in store for his future, he hopes to make use of his Comparative History of Ideas major and Global Health minor.

DIVYA RAMACHANDRA

Divya has lived all over the country, but mainly grew up in Danville, California and now lives in Madison, Wisconsin with her family. She believes she is entitled to any piece of chocolate that is around her and spends most of her time watching foreign movies. Divya's entire family is from (and mostly lives in) Bangalore and so she went on this trip to not only explore global citizenship, but to also gain a different perspective on the city her family grew up in. Besides the amazing people she met, Divya will dearly miss hailing auto rickshaws and singing Disney songs on the bus.

FABIOLA ARROYO LOPEZ

Fabiola is a junior at the University of Washington pursuing a double degree in Business Administration and Biology. She is a proud Chicana activist who uses her privilege of being in higher education to fight the injustices facing Raza and underrepresented communities. She is co-chair of ME-ChA de UW (Movimiento Estudantil Chicano/as de Aztlan), ASUW La Raza Commission Assistant Director, and Lead Ambassador for the UW Office of Minority Affairs & Diversity Recruitment & Outreach.

JENNY HOOKER

Jenny is a myriad of contradictory adjectives. A desire to understand behavior and an obsession with consequences lead her to seek amazing programs like this one that help her learn how to ask the right questions. (Image by Cas Andersen.)

JOANNE HO

Joanne studies literature and creative writing at the University of Washington. Ideally, she would like to spend her free time writing, reading science-fiction, drinking coffee in bookstores with her fiance, and eating delicious foods all day, but she happily spends a great amount it supporting students in her campus's residence halls as a Resident Adviser, in class daydreaming, and squeezing in a few hours of sleep at night when she can! She is currently in the process of applying to several graduate programs in Higher Education and Student Affairs and planning her next adventure...

KELLI CLARK

Kelli loves Jesus and the world. After graduating from the University of Washington with an International Studies degree, she will be attending a discipleship training school at Mosaic Community Church. Long term, she just hopes to love God, love people, and hopefully see the world changed. Her other interests include: wandering around, eating cheese, founding clubs, laughing, and planning adventures.

LANDON TAN

Landon has studied science and ideas at UW. He enjoys scenic beauty, strange situations, sports, pop music, Marcello Molinaro, and conversations about how best to be a person. Landon is a life-long writer and traveler.

MARCELLO MOLINARO

Marcello studies Environmental Science and enjoys hiking, backpacking, and generally being dirty. He also studies Italian and likes eating Italian as well. He will continue to do these things after he graduates this winter.

MARGARET BABAYAN

Margaret is a third-year at the University of Washington studying public health, Russian language, and human rights. For the time being, she is an undergraduate who uses any time not spent studying to sing, go on runs, and do what she hopes is good work with Amnesty International. She wants to pursue a graduate double degree in law and public health with plans to continue on toward earning a doctorate in public health.

MARIE HIGINBOTHAM

Marie is a junior studying biochemistry. She has no idea what she'll do when she graduates, but she hopes to use what she learned on this trip to somehow do good work.

MINJUNG KIM

Minjung Kim is a sophomore majoring in Bioengineering. She is in denial of the inevitable called the future and is very glad to be a sophomore for the time being. She hopes to use the next two years to find areas where social justice and bioengineering overlap. In her spare time, she dabbles in muscle mechanics research, watches films, rollerblades, and longboards.

NICOLE OKADA

Nicole is a senior studying Public Health and Bioethics. She has been deeply influenced by her travels in Kenya and Mexico, and intends to use this passion for global engagement throughout her future career in medicine.

OLIVIA LA FOND

Olivia enjoys singing, biking, and cooking/baking new recipes in her spare time. She can often be found daydreaming about her future travel plans, holding a cup of coffee, or laughing with her family and friends. Olivia is a junior at the University of Washington majoring in Communication and minoring in Global Health, and hopes to pursue non profit management in the future.

RASAN CHERALA

Rasan is a junior studying Medical Anthropology, Global Health and Biology at the University of Washington. This study abroad gave him an opportunity for self-exploration; thinking about many aspects of his life that he had never questioned living in the US and in India. Though he may come off as serious, he loves nothing more than to sit down and have a good laugh with a great group of friends. In his free time he enjoys writing, working out with his friends, and volunteering. His goal is to work as a doctor providing holistic care for people in resource deprived settings.

REBEKAH LESTER

Rebekah studies English at the UW. She likes to play music and read books when in school, and run around in rural places when she is not. Other than wanting to travel everywhere, she doesn't have much of an idea of what to do after college. She usually thinks about things that bother her, so she might try and pursue something in the realm of social justice.

RUKIE HARTMAN

Rukie is a frequent quoter of bell hooks and an experienced study abroad student. She recently graduated with degrees in Anthropology and Gender, Women and Sexuality Studies from the University of Washington. She hopes to put her critical and generous pedagogy into practice as she pursues work in higher education.

SASHA D.

Silly. Shy. Sassy. Sasha spends a lot of time thinking- about people, stories, art, identity, being, breathing. Sasha recently graduated from the University of Washington with a degree in English, and is now forced to practice as much doing as thinking.

SIMON BORUMAND

Simon is a sophomore at the University of Washington. He enjoys reading and writing and spending time with his dog Murphy. He is also a member of Sigma Chi Fraternity.

VINNIE TRAN

Vinnie is a graduating senior with a double degree in Biology and Comparative History of Ideas, and a minor in Global Health. She plans on pursuing a Masters in Public Health, hopefully at the University of Washington.

Photo Credits for book interior:
Amy Hersh, Amy Hirayama, Annika Van Gilder, Brandon Maust, Fabiola Arroyo Lopez, Kelli Clark, Margaret Babayan, Nicole Okada, Olivia Lafond, Rukie Hartman

MEET THE PROGRAM GUIDES

AMY HIRAYAMA

Amy is an 8th grade public school teacher in Seattle, Washington who uses Literature and Language Arts as vehicles for expression, connection, and change.

BRANDON MAUST

Brandon is an aspiring Pediatrician studying Medicine at the University of Washington. He has been lucky to balance the left-brain fulfillment of a career in HIV research with many collaborations for social justice.

ANU TARANATH

Anu is a speaker, facilitator, and educator who works on social justice and global issues. For more on her, please see her bio on the back cover.

GRATITUDE

IN INDIA

Hengasara Hakkina Sangha
        Ms. Indhu Subramaniam; Ms. Usha B.N.

Environment Support Group
        Mr. Leo Saldanha; Ms. Bhargavi S. Rao; Mr. K.R. Mallesh;
        Ms. Sashikala Iyer; Mr. Davis Thomas; Mr. Abhayraj Naik;
        Ms. Susheelamma

Centre for Community Dialogue and Change
        Dr. Radha Ramaswamy; Dr. P.S. Ramaswamy; Mr. Ravi Ramas-
        wamy

United Theological College
        Mr. E.J.H. Vailshery, Mr. K.V. Mathew and main office staff;
        Ms. Vasanthi, Mr. Naveen, Mr. Satish and the entire ERC
        kitchen and facilities staff

Guru Travels
        Mr. Mahesh, office staff and drivers

Mobility India
        Mr. Hemanth Kumar, Ms. Albina Shankar and kitchen, front
        office and facilities staff

Garment and Trade Workers Union
        Mrs. Madina Taj, Mrs. Ratnamma G.M.; Mrs. Ratnamma K.P.

LesBIT
        Mr. Sunil; Ms. Sumathi

Payana
        Ms. Chandini; Mr. Rex and associates

Pedestrian Pictures
      Mr. Deepak

Bangalore Walks
      Mr. Arun Pai

Shristi School of Art, Design and Technology
      Mr. Deepak Srinivasan

Nanjangud Okkuta
      Nanjangud Federation leadership and members

Mysore Mahila Samakhya
      Leadership and members

Students from Azim Premji University and Mount Carmel College

Colleagues, Friends and Well-wishers
      Mrs. Laxmi Chandrashekar; Mr. K.K.S. Murthy; Mr. Madhusud-
      han; Dr. Mrinalini Sebastian; Dr. Tejaswini Niranjana and
      Dr. Ashish Rajadhyaksha; Mr. B. Suresha; Women's Dalit Fed-
      eration in Belgaum; Mr. Mahadevan

Homestay Families:
      Mrs. Kalpana and Miss Malvika; Mrs. Asima, Mr. Ashish
      Kumar, Mr. Adil and Miss Ayesha; Mrs. Sumathi , Mr. Mohan
      Kumar, and Mr. Hemanth; Mrs. Thunga and Mr. K.R. Ramach-
      andraiah; Mrs. Kumuda Raman, Miss Sharada Raman and
      Chili the dog; Mrs. Asha Latha, Mr. Sreenivasalu and
      Miss Pragathi; Mrs. Lalitha Vijayraghavan and Mr. Vijay.

AT's Family
      Mr. P.R. Ananda Murthy; Mrs. Kusuma Murthy; Mrs. Vaishali
      Yedur, Mr. Uday Yedur; Mr. Mihir Yedur; Dr. Kamali Rao;
      Mr. P.N.A.P. Rao; Mrs. Prabha Sudhakar; Mr. H.S. Rao; Mr.
      Sandeep Rao; Mrs. Shamala Prasanna; Mr. Prasanna Bun-
      gale; Mrs. Parimala Bhargava; Mr. H.R. Bhargava

IN THE UNITED STATES

Friends, Mentors, Colleagues and Well-wishers from the University of Washington:

Betty Schmitz; Michelle Liu; Beth Kalikoff; Suhanthie Motha; Manka Varghese; Julie Villegas Maria Elena Garcia; Cynthia Anderson; Amy Peloff; Tim Cahill; Priti Ramamurthy; Keith Snodgrass; Gary Handwerk; Rachel Chapman; Tikka Sears; Miriam Bartha; Theresa Ronquillo; Shawn Wong; Nick Barr Clingan; Nara Hohensee; Erin Clowes; Christina Wygnant; John Toews; Phillip Thurtle; Jeanette Bushnell; Tamara Myers; Ed Taylor; Mike Renes; Peter Moran; Wayne Au; Rick Roth; Matthew Sparke; Deepa Rao; Carolyn Allen; John Webster; Anis Bawarshi; Frances McCue; Juan Guerra; Chandan Reddy; Candice Rai; Elizabeth Simmons-O'Neill; UW POC staff & faculty group; and a special note of thanks to the UW Seattle English department staff members for their hard work, kindness and cheer.

Friends, Family and Well-wishers:

Saroja Taranath; Bungale S. Taranath; Rajesh PN Rao; Anika Tara and Kavi Ziya; Bhavna Shamasunder; Tram Nguyen; Tamera Marko; Shazia Rahman; Vega Subramaniam; Mala Nagarajan; Sahar Romani; Sandra Gresl; Beth Rayfield; Achashman Tekle; Amy Hirayama; Brandon Maust; Susan and Gary Hirayama; Nafisa Bhojwala and Eshwar Somashekar; Smitha Rao and family; Chen Lin; Amir Sheikh; Ammara Kimso, Rochelle Tuitagava'a Fonoti, May Lukens and the AANAPISI Center's VOICES 3 community from South Seattle College; Nalini Iyer; Max Savishinsky; Laura Adriance and Tese Wintz Neighbor; Juan Carlos Astorga; Minal Hajratwala; David Fenner; Theron Stevenson; Rosemary George; Lisa Lowe; Ms. Fauzia and Ms. Seema from Travel Net; Thomas Nolet, Peter Davenport and the Hands for a Bridge Community; Zaki Abdelhamid; Rita Meher; Anjulie Ganti; Kathy Hsieh, Kathryn Flores, Shaula Messena and Guillermo Carvajal; former students who are now family friends — Emily Lee, Charmila Ajmera, Rafael

Velazquez, Saara Ahmed, Zahra Lutfeali, Melanie Robinson, Minh Nguyen, Anthony Heimuli, Sarah Moon, Amanda Morrison, DeAnn Alcantara Thompson, Alia Ahmed, Natasha Merchant and M. Abbas Rizvi; special thanks to Sasha Duttchoudury and Rukie Hartman-Thomas for enthusiastic assistance in putting together this book.

For shepherding this book into being with love and wisdom,

warm thanks to Flying Chickadee co-founders Shirin Subhani and Shahana Dattagupta.

Made in the USA
Charleston, SC
05 May 2014